Praise for *Pearl Harbor*

"There is no shortage of historical li............ .. .. attack on Pearl Harbor, so it is a brave historian who seeks to find a new way to present a familiar story. The great merit of Takuma Melber's new book on the battle is his access to Japanese sources and literature. This is the dimension commonly missing in most accounts, and it gives Melber the opportunity to provide a fuller, more definitive, and authoritative account of the battle, its background, and its consequences. Melber writes with great economy on a big subject, and he writes with flair and precision; his book is a literary achievement as well as a work of exceptional scholarship."

Richard Overy, University of Exeter

"Melber is clearly on top of his subject matter, having mastered the story of Pearl Harbor from the perspectives of both Japan and the United States. He offers fascinating new insights into what led to the attack on Pearl Harbor and thus to America's entry into World War II. He displays a thorough knowledge of the Japanese and American literature, and writes in a manner that is both accessible and authoritative. This is an excellent book that will find a ready readership among both university students and the general public."

Richard Bessel, University of York

"Here is a new look at the dramatic way Japan drew the United States into World War II. The drawing of additional details from a variety of Japanese sources as well as the published and archival material in English and German offers the reader an excellent and balanced introduction to a very important event."

Gerhard L. Weinberg, William Rand Kenan Jr. Professor Emeritus of History, University of North Carolina

"A penetrating study of one of the key events of the twentieth century from the Japanese rather than the usual American perspective. Melber's nuanced picture of Japanese wartime decision-making exposes the deep rifts in the country's military and civilian leadership. His clinical analysis of the diplomatic to-and-fro between Tokyo and Washington in the months before the attack lays bare the inevitable slide towards war."

The Australian

"In this vivid book, Takuma Melber breathes new life into the dramatic events that unfolded before, during, and after the 1941 attack on Pearl Harbor. By putting the Japanese attackers' perspective at the center of his account, he provides a more comprehensive and authoritative history of the battle, its background, and its consequences."

Military History

Pearl Harbor

Pearl Harbor

Japan's Attack and America's Entry into World War II

Takuma Melber

Translated by Nick Somers

polity

Originally published in German as *Pearl Harbor: Japans Angriff und der Kriegseintritt der USA* by Takuma Melber © Verlag C. H. Beck oHG, Munich 2016

This English edition © 2022 by Polity Press

Polity Press
65 Bridge Street
Cambridge CB2 1UR, UK

Polity Press
101 Station Landing
Suite 300
Medford, MA 02155, USA

ISBN-13: 978–1–5095–3720–4
ISBN-13: 978–1–5095–5491–1 (pb)

A catalogue record for this book is available from the British Library.

Library of Congress Cataloging-in-Publication Data
Names: Melber, Takuma, author. I Somers, Nick, translator.
Title: Pearl Harbor : Japan's attack and America's entry into World War II / Takuma Melber ; translated by Nick Somers.
Other titles: Pearl Harbor. English I Japan's attack and America's entry into World War II
Description: English edition. I Cambridge, UK ; Medford, MA : Polity, [2020] I "Originally published in German as Pearl Harbor: Japans Angriff und der Kriegseintritt der USA by Takuma Melber ©Verlag C. H. Beck oHG, München 2016." I Includes bibliographical references and index. I Summary: "A new account of one of the key battles of World War II told from the Japanese perspective."-- Provided by publisher.
Identifiers: LCCN 2020015550 (print) I LCCN 2020015551 (ebook) I ISBN 9781509537204 (hardback) I ISBN 9781509537211 (epub)
Subjects: LCSH: Pearl Harbor (Hawaii), Attack on, 1941. I World War, 1939-1945--Japan. I United States--Foreign relations--Japan. I Japan--Foreign relations--United States. I World War, 1939-1945--Campaigns--Pacific Area. I Pacific Area--History, Military. I Pacific Area--History, Naval. I World War, 1939-1945--United States.
Classification: LCC D767.92 .M4513 2020 (print) I LCC D767.92 (ebook) I DDC 940.54/26693--dc23
LC record available at https://lccn.loc.gov/2020015550
LC ebook record available at https://lccn.loc.gov/2020015551

Typeset in 11/13 Sabon by
Servis Filmsetting Ltd, Stockport, Cheshire
Printed and bound in Great Britain by TJ Books Ltd, Padstow, Cornwall

For further information on Polity, visit our website: politybooks.com

To my wife Vera and our son Paul Yoshi, to my parents Wilhelm and Yoshiko, and to my siblings Satoko and Makito with their families – with all my love and deepest gratitude

Contents

Prologue

After fighting the heavy swell and bad weather in the north Pacific for several days, the Japanese aircraft carrier *Kaga* arrived in position in the middle of the vast Pacific Ocean an hour before sunrise on December 7, 1941. The loud rattle of the engine mixed with the roar of the waves. A Mitsubishi A6M2 fighter aircraft, later known as the Zero, sped down the runway, its propellers spinning. Next in line was Akamatsu Yūji's plane.[1] Akamatsu was the observer-navigator in a torpedo bomber. The pilot, who was responsible for achieving a successful take off, pressed the button as usual to start the propeller engines and slowly maneuvered the plane into position. Akamatsu's aircraft, a Nakajima B5N, had a heavy and destructive payload in the form of an 800-kg torpedo. If the take off failed, all three crew members risked being blown to pieces without having left the aircraft carrier. Akamatsu always screened out any thoughts of dying as the plane took off and reached its flying altitude. As in the earlier exercises, everything went perfectly on this occasion, and Akamatsu's plane joined the 183 fighter planes and bombers in the Japanese aerial armada. "It must look like a swarm of bees," Akamatsu thought to himself. The armada formed the first attack wave on the US Pacific Fleet lying at anchor in Pearl Harbor in Hawaii. For the time being,

1

the commander had ordered radio silence, and Akamatsu could only hear the roaring of the engines many thousands of meters above the Pacific Ocean. He felt a deep inner calm, coupled with extreme concentration and a sense of exaltedness. He had little understanding of everyday political and diplomatic affairs, nor did he need any. He was a soldier, and his military training required only that he obey the orders of his superiors, who would know what was in Japan's national interests. There was one thing he did understand, however: the oil embargo imposed on Japan by the USA jeopardized the success of the Japanese expansion on the Chinese mainland.

The war, which had been waged there for several years, had become bogged down. Unlike the Russo-Japanese War of 1904/5, which saw the Japanese emerge as military victors but political losers, Tokyo's political and military decision-makers no longer wanted to be dictated to by the Western powers. Of course, their ranks included not only warmongering "hawks" but also "doves," who were attempting right up to the last moment to achieve a peaceful solution. Even as Akamatsu was flying towards the US naval base, Japanese diplomats were in Washington. But did they actually know anything of the war plans? Or was the attack meant to surprise Japan's representatives in Washington as much as their American colleagues?

Akamatsu's plane broke through the cloud cover. In the distance he could see the island of Hawaii the pilot was steering towards. The hour had come that would bring Japan glory and honor. The message from Admiral Yamamoto Isoroku passed on at the briefing by the fleet commander still resounded in his ears: the attack on Pearl Harbor would determine the survival or destruction of the entire Japanese nation. If the plan – which was completely reliant on the element of surprise – were to fail, the war would be lost before it had even started.

Akamatsu and the men in the first Japanese attack wave were aware of the significance of their mission: the surprise attack had to succeed at all costs. As they overflew the coast of the main Hawaiian island of Oahu, the bomber squadron maneuvered into formation and headed directly for its target, Pearl City harbor, and the US Pacific Fleet anchored there. Just a few moments after the Japanese navy airmen had spotted the main US navy base in the Pacific, Akamatsu received a signal informing him of their target, the Tennessee-class destroyer USS *California*, commissioned in 1921. Before Akamatsu knew it, the pilot was diving towards the majestic-looking enemy vessel. When the steel colossus came into his sights, he pressed the button at just the right moment, as he had learned through the months of training, to release the deadly torpedo. At that moment the plane came under heavy anti-aircraft fire. Akamatsu felt as if the US fleet, which had been taken completely by surprise, was directing all of its anti-aircraft fire at him and his plane. While the pilot ascended desperately in an attempt to dodge the hail of bullets, Akamatsu heard a loud explosion, and a blast wave passed through his body. Or was he imagining it? When the plane was finally out of the danger zone, Akamatsu looked back at the scene from a safe altitude. Black smoke was billowing from the USS *California*; he was fairly certain that the torpedo had found its target and penetrated the ship's hull. Akamatsu and his comrades had accomplished their mission. The crew were overwhelmed with a feeling of euphoria and spontaneously cried out a triumphant "Tennō Heika Banzai!" – Long live the Emperor of Japan! Akamatsu proudly set course for the aircraft carrier *Kaga*.

The aerial attack on Pearl Harbor on the morning of December 7, 1941, sent a shockwave through the USA and plunged Japan into a world war with fatal consequences. The military struggle between the Japanese

Empire and the United States of America for hegemony in the Asia-Pacific region had begun, and it would not end until the surrender of the Japanese armed forces in the summer of 1945.

1

The Background

The road to Pearl Harbor

On Friday, February 14, 1941, Nomura Kichisaburō made his way to the White House, residence of the US president, in Washington.[1] As a proven expert on America, the sixty-three-year-old Nomura had been appointed Japan's ambassador to the USA.[2] He had already lived in Washington from 1916 to 1918 as a naval attaché. A few years later, he returned as Japan's representative at the Washington Naval Conference.

After its victory in the Russo-Japanese War of 1904/5, Japan joined the group of major powers. The Japanese navy or *Nihon Kaigun* played a decisive role and was the military calling card of the Japanese Empire. In particular, the Battle of Tsushima (May 27/28, 1905), in which the navy commanded by Admiral Tōgō destroyed the Russian fleet, earned the country great respect. From that time on, Japan was recognized internationally as a serious naval power. Some fifteen years after this major military triumph, the Washington Naval Conference of 1921/22, at which Nomura represented the interests of the Japanese navy, agreed on a fleet ratio of 5:5:3 between the US navy, the British Royal Navy, and the *Nihon Kaigun*. According to the agreement, Japan undertook not to launch any battleships for the

following ten years. The Western powers were seeking to limit Japan's naval strength and to keep it at a
lower level than their own, in terms of both quality and
quantity, in order to preserve the balance of power in
the Pacific in their favor. This thwarted Japan's plan to
build its "Eight-Eight Fleet" (*hachihachi kantai*) – eight
new battleships and eight new cruisers – in the mid-
1920s. Just a few years later, however, the Japanese
navy was able to negotiate a more favorable ratio at the
London Naval Conference in 1930 of 10:7:7 in favor of
the USA. Japan's representatives even achieved a parity
ruling for submarines with the Anglo-American naval
forces.

When Nomura was sent back to Washington some
twenty years after his participation in the Washington
Conference, these maritime agreements were already a
dead letter. In the mid-1930s Japan withdrew from the
Washington and London treaties. A few years earlier,
it had revealed its ambitions in the Asia-Pacific region
by invading Manchuria on the Chinese mainland in
September 1931. Japan wanted to become the dominant
power in Asia, and to achieve this aim the government
in Tokyo had gradually embarked on a new political
course. Hard hit by the 1929 world economic crisis, it
had set out in a political direction determined increasingly by the military. Territorial expansion was now at
the top of Japan's foreign policy agenda. The invasion
of Manchuria, rich in iron ore, coal, and grain, was the
first step to solving Japan's own economic problems –
by acquiring new land for its growing population and
gaining access to natural resources. The members of
Japanese naval circles, who saw the results of the international naval conferences that guaranteed the balance
of power in the Pacific as a limitation on the *Nihon
Kaigun*, were making themselves increasingly heard
in public and in politics. But it was not only in naval
matters that Japan was assuming a more determined

diplomatic attitude towards the Western powers. This attitude was also reflected in foreign policy, with Japan's withdrawal in 1933 from the League of Nations, which had been established by President Woodrow Wilson as a reaction to the horrors of World War I. Japan was distancing itself increasingly from its most important naval interlocutors: Great Britain and the USA. Instead it turned to the rising German Reich and Fascist Italy – a process that culminated in the Tripartite Pact and the formation of the Rome-Berlin-Tokyo Axis in 1940. The common denominators uniting the three signatories were an aggressive foreign policy and the desire for territorial expansion. The Pact called for the signatories to assist one another in the event that any of them was attacked by a country not yet involved in the wars in Asia and Europe, notably the USA. The Axis powers also divided the world into spheres of interest: east Asia for Japan, eastern Europe for the German Reich, and the Mediterranean for Italy.

By the time Nomura started his diplomatic service in the USA in February 1941, Germany and Italy were already waging war in parts of Europe. The German Wehrmacht invaded Poland on September 1, 1939, and in summer 1940 large parts of northern and western Europe, including France and the Netherlands, were occupied by the Germans. Hitler's army also attempted to defeat Great Britain, the last major opponent in Europe. In the Mediterranean, meanwhile, Italy was pursuing its own expansion plans as Mussolini's troops engaged the forces of the British Empire in North Africa.

War had broken out in Asia earlier on. After Japan's intervention in Manchuria and the establishment of its puppet state Manchukuo, and following the Marco Polo Bridge Incident in Peking on July 7, 1937, when Chinese and Japanese soldiers exchanged fire, the Japanese armed forces were now opposed by Chinese government troops commanded by Chiang Kai-shek, and by the

Chinese communist forces. Large parts of China, particularly the north and coastal regions, were occupied
by Japan. The capital Nanking fell in December 1937.[3]
The Japanese army committed unspeakable atrocities
there and massacred thousands of Chinese civilians.
This did not by any means mark the end of the conflict.
On the contrary, the military situation in the Chinese
theatre of war soon became "bogged down."[4] Japan's
advance came to a standstill, and the conflict degen-
erated into a veritable positional war. The Japanese
army units in the hinterland met with constant resistance from Chinese guerrillas. Supplies for the Japanese
were slow in arriving, while aid from the West ensured
the survival of the Chinese troops. Overall, the war
against the Chinese was proving wearing and tough for
Japan's army. Many political and military experts in the
Japanese Empire sought an end to the hostilities – albeit
in the form of either total victory over China or a peace
treaty on Japanese terms.

When the Manchurian crisis erupted in September
1931, the then US president Herbert Hoover had
rejected the idea of sanctions against the Japanese
aggressor. Under Franklin D. Roosevelt, who succeeded
Hoover in 1933, US foreign policy in the region changed
tack – from isolation to intervention. The willingness of
the new president to remain as a bystander in the war on
the Chinese mainland had reached its limits. News of the
atrocities committed by the Japanese, combined with the
outcry in the international media, persuaded Roosevelt
and his government to oppose Japanese expansion and
side with China. The decision was prompted not only
by humanitarian considerations, however, but also by
the desire to safeguard the influence of the USA in Asia
and, in particular, to protect US economic interests.
Roosevelt sought to achieve these aims not by force
of arms but through economic pressure on Japan. The
first step was taken in 1939, when the US government

announced its intention not to renew the US-Japanese trade treaty established in 1911 and due to expire the following year. This measure had its impact, given that the Japanese economy was highly reliant on the USA. The previous year, Japan had exported 23 percent of its goods there, and 34 percent of its imports – including more than half of its imported oil, iron, and steel – came from the USA.[5] In spite of the cancelation of the trade treaty, Japan still sought to establish its hegemony on the Chinese mainland and to become the dominant power in Asia. This course of aggressive expansion was to be continued. The Open Door Policy pursued by the Americans since the late nineteenth century – designed to give the USA, the European colonial powers, and the Japanese Empire equal access to China as a trading partner and market – had already been rejected by the Japanese government in 1938. In March 1940, Japan installed a new pro-Japanese government in China, led by Wang Jingwei.[6] The US government responded by granting loans worth millions of dollars to the Chinese nationalist government in support of Chiang Kai-shek. After the success of the German Wehrmacht campaign in the west, culminating in the fall of Paris and the occupation of France, Japan exerted pressure on the Dutch government in exile in London to obtain oil from the Dutch East Indies, its colony in Asia. It was also authorized by the pro-German Vichy government in France to station its fighter units in French Indochina so as to be able to launch aerial attacks on central China from there. In September 1940 Japanese troops even occupied the north of French Indochina so as to gain access to its natural resources and to block an important Anglo-American supply route to Chiang Kai-shek. They hoped in this way to be able to end the war in China. The reaction of the major European powers was not long in coming, however. Great Britain resumed the halted provision of supplies to China via the Burma Road. The

US government also stepped up its financial support for China and introduced an embargo in mid-October 1940 that drastically limited deliveries of scrap iron and metal and other vital goods, including aircraft fuel, from the USA to Japan. A total oil embargo, as demanded by hardliners such as Secretary of War Henry L. Stimson and Secretary of the Treasury Henry Morgenthau, was not instituted. Even in 1940, Japan obtained over 90 percent of its oil from the USA.[7] The advocates of a more moderate course still held sway, in particular Secretary of State Cordell Hull and Under Secretary of State Benjamin Sumner Welles, supported by representatives of the US navy. They sought at all costs to avoid provoking the Japanese into a panicked military response.

A mood of crisis thus prevailed between Japan and the USA when the Japanese government sent Nomura to Washington as ambassador in early 1941. In particular, the "China question," the resolution of the military conflict on the Chinese mainland, which had hardened into an unyielding positional war, put a great strain on bilateral relations. At the time, therefore, it was not in Japan's interests to exacerbate the diplomatic ill feeling between Japan and the USA to the point of making a military conflict inevitable. Ambassador Nomura's priority was thus to prevent a war between the two countries.

Nomura, who, after a career in the imperial navy, regarded himself more as a military man than a diplomat, entered the White House on February 14, 1941, to present his credentials as Japanese ambassador to President Roosevelt. The meeting was cordial enough: Nomura and Roosevelt, who had been elected president for the third time in November 1940, were old acquaintances, even friends. They had met when Nomura was a naval attaché in Washington during World War I and Roosevelt was Assistant Secretary of the Navy. After

Nomura's return to Japan, the two had continued a friendly correspondence by mail. Their correspondence reveals, for example, the great regret expressed by them both at not being able to meet in New York in 1929, when Roosevelt was governor and Nomura was visiting the city.[8] Nomura had also extended several invitations to his friend to visit him in Japan. In a letter of April 6, 1937, Roosevelt wrote: "I hope the day will come when I can visit Japan. I have much interest in the great accomplishments of the Japanese people and I should much like to see many of my Japanese friends again."[9] Since contracting polio in 1921, however, Roosevelt had been confined to a wheelchair, which considerably restricted his possibilities for travel. Japan's hope for finding a solution to the tense bilateral relations was thus understandably dependent to a large extent on the good personal contact between the two now elderly men.[10]

A few days after the friendly reunion with Roosevelt, the Japanese ambassador visited another old acquaintance in Washington. US Secretary of State Cordell Hull met Nomura in the latter's apartment in the luxury Carlton hotel, which the Japanese ambassador had preferred to the official headquarters of the State Department, so as to enable the two men to conduct exploratory talks out of the public eye. Hull was an experienced politician, but Nomura had much greater difficulty in understanding him than he did Roosevelt on account of Hull's strong Southern accent.[11] He was nevertheless very familiar with the department headed by Hull since 1933, as he himself had been Japanese foreign minister in 1939/40. At their first meeting on March 8, 1941, Hull and Nomura clearly stated the reason for the ill feeling between Japan and the USA, namely the US embargo and Japan's resultant economic problems. Hull asked specifically whether Japan intended to continue to expand in south-east Asia towards the British stronghold of Singapore and the Dutch East Indies. Nomura denied this, although he added "unless it cannot be avoided."[12] Although Nomura was in Washington to seek a peaceful solution to the simmering conflict through diplomatic channels, he could not and did not wish to make any promises to the Americans, not least as there were many advocates back home, particularly in military circles, of *nanshinron* – territorial expansion to the south. In their view, the advances by the Japanese army to date had not gone far enough. Moreover, south-east Asia's natural resources were lucrative targets of further expansion, particularly in view of the US embargo. Nomura was well aware of this situation.

The Americans believed, however, that the expansion

February 1941: US Secretary of State Cordell Hull and the Japanese ambassador Nomura Kichisaburō meeting in Washington to seek a solution to the American-Japanese conflict.
Underwood Archives/UIG/Bridgeman Images

in south-east Asia was more likely to be motivated by the Axis treaty with the German Reich and Italy than by the US embargo, as Hull made clear to the Japanese ambassador. At a further meeting in the White House, Roosevelt and Hull emphasized to Nomura that the Japanese Empire must state explicitly that its desire for more influence in Asia was of a purely economic nature. It should demonstrate that it did not intend to expand so as to gain exclusive access to oil in the Dutch East Indies or rubber in the Malayan peninsula by taking possession of those territories.[13]

This clear exposition of the problems gave new impetus in April 1941 to exploratory American-Japanese talks, which Nomura interpreted as a preliminary to official bilateral negotiations. Private parties from both countries submitted a draft proposal to the State Department as a basis for those negotiations. It demanded an end to the war in China and the implementation of the Open Door Policy.

Although Hull was essentially in agreement with the proposal, he considered that its vague formulation left considerable scope for interpretation. When and to what extent would Japan withdraw its troops from China? And did Washington and Tokyo mean the same thing by the Open Door Policy?[14] These were just two of the questions posed by Hull, who sought in further talks with Nomura to clarify the proposal. He made it apparent that negotiations could be officially started only after acceptance of four Basic Principles: first, a guarantee of the territorial integrity and sovereignty of all nations; second, non-interference in the internal affairs of other countries; third, continued priority for the principle of equality – for example, in terms of economic prospects – and hence the postulate of the Open Door Policy; and fourth, maintenance of the status quo in the Pacific, unless changes were made by peaceful means.[15] Hull, who had announced early on that "we do not make peace with Japan at the expense of China,"[16] dashed any hopes held by Japan that the USA would officially recognize its territorial gains in China achieved by military force. At the same time, the Basic Principles were also an indication of the Americans' desire to resolve the crisis in the Far East by peaceful rather than military means. They saw the Principles as an offer to the Japanese to come over to the American side. Hull was aware that he had a very small margin to work with: US concessions should not be so generous as to allow Japan to accept them and then interpret them at a more propitious date as justification for further expansion. In early 1941, however, Hull believed that "as long as Britain stoutly resisted Germany and at the same time the American fleet remained in the Pacific, [Japan] would try to nibble off what she could without engaging in a major conflict."[17] He nevertheless endeavored to avoid any further drastic economic or military measures that would provoke a direct war with Japan. Open hostility towards the Japanese Empire was not in the interests of the USA and had to be prevented – in part to enable it to concentrate on the conflict with the German Reich, with which it was not yet at war.

In its inter-war military plans, the strategists in Washington had set great store by War Plan Orange, which focused on Japan as the sole adversary and called for the transfer of the Atlantic Fleet to the Pacific in the event of a war, to enable the USA to engage in a decisive battle with the Japanese navy following the deployment of its Combined Fleet.[18] However, in reaction to Hitler's aggressive European policy in 1938 and 1939, which resulted in the territorial expansion of the German Reich through the annexation of Austria, the incorporation of the Sudetenland and the occupation of Czechoslovakia, American military strategists substantially modified their operative guidelines. After the Wehrmacht occupied large parts of Europe in 1939 and

1940 and was preparing to invade the British Isles, the Americans increasingly regarded the German Reich as potentially the most serious threat to their own country and to world peace. In June 1940, Roosevelt therefore asked his chief army and navy planners to develop a strategy based on the premise of Germany continuing to threaten Great Britain. The Plan Dog memorandum by Chief of Naval Operations Admiral Harold R. Stark in November 1940 stated that in the event of a war on two fronts, with Germany and Japan, Great Britain should be offered every conceivable form of military support – including the deployment of troops by land, sea, and air. The US armed forces should be in a position first and foremost to carry out offensive operations against the German Reich, while the attitude to Japan should be defensive.[19]

British and American military planners met in early 1941 to discuss a joint strategy on the basis of Admiral Stark's memorandum, in the event that the USA should enter the war. The US government avoided giving the British a specific assurance of military assistance, while the United Kingdom requested in vain that the US Pacific Fleet be based in Manila so that it would be in a better position to protect Singapore. The US government considered its reaction to Japan's expansion the previous year to be adequate. After the annual maneuvers in May 1940, the Pacific Fleet did not return to the West Coast but to Pearl Harbor on the island of Hawaii and hence to a forward position in the Pacific. Even a year later, the Americans regarded this military presence in the Pacific as a sufficient deterrent to further territorial encroachments by Japan in south-east Asia and hence to an unbounded conflict in the Pacific.[20] It was for that reason as well that Roosevelt refused a request from Admiral James Otto Richardson, commander of the US Pacific Fleet, to return the fleet to the West Coast for logistical reasons. This move could have been regarded by the Japanese as a retreat, and neither Roosevelt nor his diplomats wanted under any circumstances to show any sign of weakness.[21]

In April 1941, the US military strategists finally devised the "Rainbow 5" plan, one of several evolving "rainbow plans" considering US involvement in a war on multiple fronts. It provided for parallel US combat against Japan in the Pacific and against the German Reich in the Atlantic. The USA and Great Britain would fight side by side in a coalition, with the US armed forces concentrating on offensive operations in Europe and Africa.[22] The Germany-first strategy later advanced by the Allies, which gave priority to defeating the German threat over a war with Japan, was thus already effectively established at this early stage. The authorities not only in London but also in Washington were focusing on the war in Europe and on the German Reich as the main threat to world peace. As such, the Asia-Pacific region played only a subordinate role in their war plans. The Americans wished to avoid combat with Japan as far as possible. The highest priority was accorded to defending the Atlantic and protecting maritime links with Europe and the entire western hemisphere, which were seen as a lifeline.

While Nomura was attempting to set up official negotiations in Washington in early 1941, the government in Tokyo was intent at the same time on keeping his exploratory talks secret, in view of the great danger that the German Reich and Italy would misinterpret official Japanese-American negotiations as a rejection of the Tripartite Pact. Moreover, the supporters of the Axis regarded the Principles presented by Hull as a prerequisite for bilateral consultations as conflicting with the Tripartite Pact. If Japan were to agree to the US Principles, its expansion policy would be stopped. In addition, an American-Japanese agreement of this nature could result in British and American troops being transferred from the south-west Pacific to the war in Europe, where in early 1941 the military confrontation between Great Britain and Nazi Germany was well established. Although the USA had not yet joined the war on the side of Prime Minister Winston Churchill, it was nevertheless providing logistical support to the British Empire. For foreign minister Matsuoka Yōsuke, in early 1941, the allegiances were clear, and an American-Japanese agreement would fundamentally jeopardize the Tripartite Pact. Ambassador Nomura saw things differently: in his eyes an agreement with the USA would offer Japan a chance to considerably improve its situation, giving it access to urgently required natural resources that would enable it to put an end to the stalled war with China. In addition, he wrote in a telegram to Matsuoka:

> By this proposal [an understanding between Japan and the USA] . . . the danger of a conflict between the United States and Germany will be lessened. On the other hand, granted that after the establishment of this understanding the United States will give more assistance to Great Britain, our Empire will be able thereby all the better to restrain the United States from participating in the European war. This coincides with our duty to support Germany in her desire to have no trouble with the United States and strengthen the spirit of the Tripartite Treaty. If this proposal is accepted, our Empire's right to speak in the international situation will be greater than ever.[23]

For Nomura, who was convinced that, after coming to an arrangement with Japan, the USA would remain neutral and not side with Great Britain in the war, an agreement with the United States was quite consistent with the Tripartite Pact. If the talks with Hull were to come to nothing, however, then war between the Axis and the USA in Europe and the Asia-Pacific region would be inevitable.[24]

While Nomura in Washington sought a Japanese-American rapprochement and the start of official reconciliation negotiations, Matsuoka set off on a trip to Europe. He had been appointed foreign minister in July 1940 as part of the cabinet formed by Prime Minister Konoe Fumimaro and had been a well-known supporter of ultra-nationalist ideas for years. On February 25, 1933, he had energetically rebuffed international protests at the League of Nations in Geneva against Japan's expansion on the Chinese mainland. He claimed that anarchy reigned in neighboring China, and that the Japanese army had invaded the country to restore order and to help Manchuria gain the independence it supposedly sought. When forty-two nations refused to recognize Japan's puppet state Manchukuo, however, Matsuoka stormed out of the packed Geneva conference room in a rage, together with the entire Japanese delegation. Japan then withdrew from the League of Nations and ended its international cooperation. In order to counter Japan's resultant isolation, Matsuoka became a voluble supporter of an alliance with Nazi Germany, which had also left the League of Nations in 1933. Just a few weeks after Matsuoka became foreign minister, Japan concluded the Tripartite Pact in September 1940. The treaty alliance concluded a few years before with the German Reich – which in early 1938 had ceased to support China and sided clearly with Japan in the Sino-Japanese conflict – now also included Fascist Italy. Matsuoka saw this alliance, the Rome-Berlin-Tokyo Axis, as a "military alliance aimed at the USA."[25] As he wrote in an essay published in May 1940, he was convinced that a confrontation between Japan and the USA was inevitable as long as the two powers did not mutually respect their respective spheres of influence and did not cooperate with one another.[26] The conclusion of the Tripartite Pact clearly defined the foreign policy fronts. For Matsuoka, the British and Americans were Japan's enemies.

The state visits by Matsuoka in late March 1941, during which he met Hitler, von Ribbentrop, and Göring in Berlin and leading representatives of the Fascist regime in Rome,[27] were above all a symbolic publicity act. They confirmed the ties within the alliance, as the Axis propaganda was not slow to emphasize. Of much greater importance was another stop on Matsuoka's trip. Instead of passing through the USA on his way home, as Nomura had suggested, to give a sign of good-will and of Japan's peaceful intentions,[28] the Japanese foreign minister visited Moscow. The signing there, on April 13, of a five-year Japanese-Soviet Neutrality Pact was a veritable foreign policy coup. Less than two years previously, the armies of the two countries had faced each other at the border of Manchuria and Russia, when the Japanese Empire had attempted in summer 1939 to expand its territory to the north. As Matsuoka stated to Kido Kōichi, Lord Keeper of the Privy Seal and a close adviser to the Emperor, before leaving for Europe, after the regulation of Soviet-Japanese relations, his foreign policy masterplan in early 1941 called for achieving peace with China and then "concentrating all forces and turning southward."[29] For supporters of *nanshinron*, expansion in south-east Asia, an agreement of this nature with the Soviet Union was a vital prerequisite. With Russia's neutrality guaranteed, Japanese units could be withdrawn from the border region of Manchuria and Russia to reinforce military capacities in the advance in a southerly direction with a view to gaining access to natural resources. In Washington as well, the Japanese-Soviet Neutrality Pact suggested that Japan was at least considering expanding in south-east Asia in the near future. The Pact was also interpreted as a possible preliminary to the addition of the Soviet Union to the Tripartite Pact so as to deter the Western powers from intervening in the Far East while Japan constructed its Greater East Asian Empire. The

Neutrality Pact of April 1941 clearly rang alarm bells for the authorities in Washington.

American suspicions were reinforced not only by the result of Matsuoka's six-week trip but also by his direct attitude to the USA: even after his return from Europe on April 22 he still failed to respond to the four Basic Principles proposed by Hull.[30]

Four days previously, the foreign ministry in Tokyo had received a telegram from Nomura summarizing his talks in Washington and containing a first American draft version of a Japanese-American treaty. It touched on the issues of recognition of Manchukuo, the merging of the Chiang Kai-shek and Wang Jingwei governments to put an end to the military conflict in China, and normalization of trade relations. Although the draft was still very vague, it was intended as the basis for the first official talks – as Nomura emphasized to the Japanese foreign ministry – so as to bring the disputing parties to the negotiating table.[31]

For some reason Matsuoka seemed to be playing for time, and Nomura already feared that the foreign minister's delaying tactic could compromise his own credibility with the Americans.[32] To Hull as well, his Japanese counterpart minister also appeared uncooperative, not least after Matsuoka's antics in Tokyo did the rounds in Washington. Just a few days after his return, Matsuoka gave a speech in the Hibiya Public Hall, close to the imperial palace, in which he described Italy and particularly the German Reich – with its economic, military, and political strength and above all its resolute confrontation of the Western powers – as an exemplary model for his own country. Expressing great admiration he announced that "the Duce Mussolini and the Führer Hitler are so close that not a drop of water could be placed between them."[33] His meeting with Stalin and Molotov, which culminated in the signing of the Japanese-Soviet Neutrality Pact, was also mentioned in glowing terms. He was lavish in his praise of Hitler, Stalin, and Mussolini as strong leaders of totalitarian and hence antidemocratic regimes, in contrast to Japan, weakly led by Prime Minister Konoe. All of the USA's ideological enemies featured prominently in Matsuoka's speech.[34] In the light of these utterances by Matsuoka – the most important official representative of Japanese foreign policy – it is understandable that the Americans should have gained the impression that Japan was positioning itself in opposition to the USA. In this early phase of the exploratory talks, the positioning of the Japanese actors on the diplomatic stage posed an appreciable problem. While Nomura in Washington was evidently seeking a rapprochement with the USA, Matsuoka in Japan was coming out with aggressive slogans that demonstrated an undying faith in the Tripartite Pact. To the State Department in Washington, well informed of the Japanese foreign minister's activities, Japan's diplomacy seemed contradictory, and the Americans were unable to discern a clear line in Japanese foreign policy.

The patience of Hull and Nomura, who were waiting expectantly for a reaction from Tokyo to the four Basic Principles, was already tried almost to the limit when the Japanese embassy in Washington finally received a telegram from the Japanese foreign ministry (*Gaimushō*). Matsuoka suggested an agreement with the USA in the form of a bilateral neutrality pact similar to the one he had negotiated with the Soviet Union. He informed Nomura in the telegram that he had in mind an agreement with the USA that he could sell in Japan as "a sort of diplomatic blitzkrieg"[35] and a great foreign policy achievement. Hull rejected this rather clumsy proposal without further ado. Agreeing to a neutrality pact – in Hull's view a completely useless instrument that would be of no help in solving the existing problems – would be a clear concession to Japan and a defeat for the US government. It would be tantamount to abandoning the four Basic Principles, which, as he insisted to Nomura, must continue to form the basis for Japanese-American talks. Moreover, a neutrality pact of this nature would be interpreted as effectively a recognition by the USA of Japan's territorial gains in China achieved by force.[36]

When the "China question" became the focus of the talks in mid-May 1941, a genuine rapprochement between the two countries appeared possible. In the hope that the United States would act as a mediator between the warring parties, as it had done in the Russo-Japanese War of 1904/5, Japan asked the USA to exert its influence on Chiang Kai-shek, commander of the Chinese government forces, by threatening to cut off all support if the Chinese government in Chungking was not willing to enter into peace negotiations with Japan. According to a memorandum from the Japanese foreign ministry, the Matsuoka Plan, as it was called – or the May 12 Plan, for the date it was sent by Nomura to Hull – the peace terms should be based on the "principles of the Konoe government":[37] first, the friendly neighbor principle; second, the formation of a "united front" against the communist threat in the north; and third, the principle of economic cooperation. The specific proposal called for economic cooperation between Japan and the USA in the south Pacific. Although the withdrawal of Japanese troops on the basis of a future Sino-Japanese agreement was posited, the memorandum continued to insist on the independence of Manchukuo and Japan's adherence to the Tripartite Pact, and included a clause designed to deter other countries – specifically the USA – from entering the war in Europe. Matsuoka's clear intention was the uncompromising and tenacious defense of a position of strength vis-à-vis Washington. As he said to Nomura, for Japan good relations with the USA were of comparatively subordinate significance, and the main thrust of his foreign policy was implementation of the Tripartite Pact. Japan must therefore endeavor to deter the USA from taking action against the Axis powers or from entering the war in Europe at all. Still under the influence of his visit to Europe, in May 1941 Matsuoka even advocated an advance southward by the Japanese army to capture the British stronghold of Singapore in compliance with the demands of the commanders-in-chief of the German air force and navy, Hermann Göring and Erich Raeder.[38] Matsuoka believed that "if Britain surrenders [to Japan] an hour *before* the United States enters the war in Europe, the United States will change its mind and refrain from going to war."[39] At all events it was necessary to avoid giving the impression that Japan would not attack the United States if the USA went to war with the German Reich. In early summer 1941, Matsuoka was quite intentionally rattling his samurai sword.

In bilateral discussions with Nomura in May, Hull expressed his willingness to persuade Chiang Kai-shek to enter into peace negotiations – a clear indication that the Americans saw a reconciliation between China and Japan as a basic prerequisite for peace in the Pacific in general. He believed that once an agreement had been reached between China and Japan, all of the other points in the Japanese proposal could be somehow settled. He nevertheless made it clear that the differences between the two proposals were quite considerable. As far as the Pacific was concerned, Japan had given no firm assurances with regard to the Basic Principles formulated by the Americans. Hull believed that Japan's refusal to withdraw from the Tripartite Pact as demanded by the USA indicated rather an intention to pursue the policy of expansion in the Pacific advocated by the Axis. Its proposed solution to the Chinese question was likewise unsatisfactory for the Americans. Nomura, who also thought that "peace in the Pacific would be the first step toward later peace in Europe,"[40] described the situation in a telegram to the *Gaimushō*: "I and my associates are certainly not optimistic, but on the other hand, we are not pessimistic."[41] He believed that the outcome of the exploratory talks was still completely open. The Americans were also uncertain as to the outcome of the talks. Hull constantly reaffirmed his willingness to find a peaceful solution. Under no circumstances did he wish to miss the opportunity of reaching an agreement with Japan, even if there was only a one in twenty-five chance of it happening, he informed Joseph C. Grew, the US ambassador in Tokyo.[42] At the same time, Hull was quite adamant about the US position. He emphasized to Nomura the three main topics of discussion. First, the USA was not willing to allow Japan to dictate its attitude to the war in Europe. On the contrary, Japan should guarantee not to oppose the USA if the United States felt obliged as a preventive defensive measure to enter the war in Europe. In other words, the US government insisted on its interpretation of the right of self-defense. Second, the USA once again opposed the stationing of Japanese troops in northern China. And third, it explicitly insisted on economic equality in China and the Pacific.

In summer 1941, an unforeseen event radically changed the situation for both parties. Operation Barbarossa, the German invasion of the Soviet Union on June 22, dashed Matsuoka's hope for a German-Italian-Soviet-Japanese alliance against Great Britain and the USA. Until then, the Japanese had not taken seriously the unequivocal German hints at an impending war in the East. Ōshima Hiroshi, Japan's ambassador in Berlin, had already indicated in April that the German Reich would launch an attack there. Allied Germany hoped, however, that Japan would not interfere in the military conflict.[43] Even when Hitler asked Ōshima indirectly for Japanese arms to assist in the imminent combat in the East, Matsuoka and minister of war Tōjō in Tokyo were still reluctant to believe that Germany would take up arms against the Soviet Union.[44] The attack therefore came as a surprise to the authorities in Tokyo as well.

How Japan would respond to this situation was initially unclear. On the one hand, it was allied with Germany, but on the other hand it had signed a Neutrality Pact with the Soviet Union only a few weeks earlier. After the German invasion of the Soviet Union, however, the position of the Japanese foreign minister changed fundamentally: having earlier been an advocate of a Japanese advance to the south, he now supported Japan's entry into war with Germany against the Soviet Union. He believed that the Wehrmacht would defeat the Soviet Red Army. He also expected Britain, the USA, and the Soviet Union to form an alliance, with the result that Japan was likely to be surrounded by Allied forces in the Pacific. Unlike Matsuoka, however, Japan's politicians and military wanted to wait to see who would be victorious in the German-Soviet conflict and not to take sides over-hastily. From Washington, Nomura, who was still in favor of concluding an agreement with the USA as rapidly as possible, requested the government in Tokyo not to take up arms in the conflict by, for example, invading Siberia. Under no circumstances did he want the bilateral talks to be jeopardized by an action of this nature. In reply, Matsuoka accused Nomura, whom he believed to be strongly influenced by the Americans, of attempting to influence the Japanese government on behalf of the Americans and of giving the impression in the USA that some members of the Konoe government were unreliable and that the Japanese cabinet was not united.

This protest by Matsuoka was to be his last intervention in the American-Japanese exploratory talks. There was indeed great disagreement in Konoe's government about the country's political direction. Just before the start of Operation Barbarossa, Prime Minister Konoe himself had expressed dissatisfaction with Matsuoka's foreign policy. In view of the impending hostilities between the German Reich and the Soviet Union, he claimed, it was even more in Japan's interests to seek a compromise with the USA.[45] He was unwilling to provoke war with the Soviet Union as well, especially in view of the adverse effects on the Japanese Empire of the war with China. Like Nomura, he also hoped that a peaceful solution could be negotiated in Washington. He told Lord Keeper of the Privy Seal Kido that the cabinet, which was split between him and Matsuoka, should draw the obvious conclusions and resign if a) the US response was not in Japan's interests, b) the USA went to war, or c) war should break out between the German Reich and the Soviet Union.[46]

In summer 1941, Konoe, who during Matsuoka's trip to Europe had attempted to isolate the warmongering foreign minister at home, considered that the time had come to get rid of him. The cabinet and the high command – which was interested in expansion in south-east Asia – had decided that Japan should wage war against the Soviet Union only at a later date, if at all, when the situation was favorable. Using the discord regarding the German-Soviet war as a pretext, and seeking to distance itself from Matsuoka – who had fallen out of favor but who still militated strongly for Japan's entry into war against the Soviet Union – Konoe's cabinet resigned on June 17, 1941.

The crisis intensifies

The formation of the new cabinet, Konoe's third, marked the start of a decisive phase, setting the scene for further developments in the Pacific. Konoe remained prime minister at the Emperor's express wish. Matsuoka's successor as foreign minister was the much more moderate Toyoda Teijirō. As former minister of trade and industry, he was well aware of Japan's precarious economic situation, which had been further exacerbated by the Allied embargo. He was inexperienced in diplomacy but was on friendly terms with Nomura after their shared time in the navy. Although Nomura himself expressed the wish on July 14 to resign from office so as to be able to influence the political situation of his country in Tokyo, the new Japanese government insisted on his remaining as its representative in Washington. Roosevelt was also aware of Nomura's good personal relationship with Toyoda and placed high hopes on the new head of the *Gaimushō*. With the departure of Matsuoka, both Nomura and Roosevelt expected a change in Japan's foreign policy.

"As the result of our negotiations with the Vichy government, we were able to come to an understanding . . . with regard to jointly defending French Indochina. . . . We are to peacefully occupy the southern part of French Indochina on or about 28 or 29 July."[47] This message from Toyoda of July 23 informed Nomura of Japan's plans in south-east Asia. The ambassador had previously strongly warned the Japanese government against a military occupation of French Indochina, which could cause the Japanese-American exploratory talks to be aborted. At the insistence of the *Gaimushō*, however, he was now required to assure the US government that the Japanese occupation was not an attack on the territorial sovereignty or the internal administration of French Indochina. Toyoda informed his friend Nomura that this territorial acquisition had been decided by the previous government.

Whereas in summer 1941 the Japanese army was still intent on avoiding war with the USA and Great Britain, in the navy the advocates of southward expansion and a mainly naval war against the Western colonial powers had gained the upper hand. The army had not supported Matsuoka's plan to attack the Soviet Union as it did not have heavy tanks – a basic prerequisite for warfare in Mongolia or Siberia. In any case, the army did not have enough manpower to wage war not only in China but also with the Soviet Union. The invasion of French Indochina, which army representatives at the time believed should be Japan's only expansion, represented a compromise for the army and navy. By advancing to French Indochina, Japan would acquire natural resources such as tin and rubber and would also bring its troops closer to British Malaya and the Dutch East Indies, which were further potential targets for Japan's territorial expansion in south-east Asia. In the short term, access to vital resources would enable the war in China to be continued and possibly concluded, as the army wished. In the long term, all options for a more extensive war would remain, either continuing southward or attacking the Soviet Union at a more favorable time – if the Red Army were to retreat, for example, westward from Asia towards Europe. And so, on July 2, at the first imperial conference (*gozen kaigi*) of 1941 – a meeting that was not in fact provided for in the Constitution, in which the country's political and military leaders discussed important foreign policy matters with the Emperor – the decision taken a few days previously by the imperial headquarters to invade the south of French Indochina was endorsed.[48]

A few days later Toyoda informed his ambassador in Washington that he had not yet had the time to formulate the guidelines for his own foreign policy, but explicitly desired that the talks between Hull and Nomura continue. He was interested in particular in dissuading the USA from taking anti-Japanese measures as a reaction to the effective occupation of French Indochina by Japan. For Toyoda this was "a matter of necessity for the fact of peace in the Pacific."[49] He told Nomura of his firm belief that an American reaction, such as the freezing of Japanese assets or an oil embargo, would have an extremely adverse effect on bilateral relations. If that were to occur, Tokyo would be forced to take countermeasures – hence the need to deter Roosevelt and Hull from taking such steps.

In a series of discussions, Japan's diplomatic representatives attempted to justify to Washington the invasion of French Indochina. They claimed first that it was a matter of self-defense. There was an increasing belief in Japan that, following the outbreak of hostilities between the German Reich and the Soviet Union, the country risked being encircled by the USA, the Soviet Union, Great Britain, and the Netherlands. Second, the stationing of Japanese troops in French Indochina was also justified for economic reasons, they said, as it was the only way of ensuring Japan's access to vital natural resources. According to the Americans, however, the Japanese advance was prompted less by economic considerations than by pressure from Germany. Under Secretary of State Sumner Welles, one of Roosevelt's most important foreign policy advisers, had already advised the US president in early July to order a comprehensive economic embargo of Japan if it were to use the outbreak of war between the German Reich and the Soviet Union as a pretext for further expansion.[50] But in spite of this advice, and unmoved by the growing public outcry for massive restrictions, Roosevelt did not immediately stop ongoing deliveries, including oil, to Japan. On the contrary, at a meeting on July 24 he made Nomura an offer, one that was strongly criticized by Welles, who was also present.[51] In return for the withdrawal of Japanese troops from French Indochina, he proposed a treaty with Japan, Great Britain, China, the Netherlands, and, of course, the USA itself. Roosevelt secretly believed that Hitler had incited Japan to further expansion. The treaty with these countries would guarantee larger quantities of the necessary natural resources at lower cost than would be possible through the military occupation of French Indochina, which should be treated as a neutral territory – like Switzerland, which Roosevelt explicitly cited as an example – whose natural resources could be shared by the signatories to such a treaty. As a foreign policy aim, Roosevelt sought to make the renunciation of any military intervention in Asia and the respect for state autonomy as a "Good Neighbor Policy" into a central focus of his presidency. This policy had already been successfully implemented in Central and South America. Now Roosevelt attempted to persuade Nomura of the advantages of the Good Neighbor Policy in Asia. The Japanese ambassador, who emphasized to Roosevelt that he personally regretted the Japanese expansion in French Indochina, was not very optimistic. A public concession to the USA in the form of a troop withdrawal would represent an enormous loss of face for the Japanese nation and was hence a step that the government and, in particular, the ultra-right and pro-military circles, who were in favor of war, would not accept under any circumstances.

On July 25, 1941, just a day after Nomura's meeting with Roosevelt, the USA began to freeze Japanese assets as a reaction to the stationing of Japanese troops in French Indochina. Great Britain followed suit a short while afterwards.[52] On July 26 the US president signed an Executive Order bringing "all financial and import and export trade transactions in which Japanese interests are involved under the control of the government."[53] The American reaction also included a comprehensive export embargo on American goods to Japan, including vital oil exports. With its great dependency on imports, Japan was hard hit, since 90 percent of its oil came from abroad, three-quarters of that from the USA.[54] The Japanese government reacted to Roosevelt's freezing order by itself freezing American assets.

The diplomatic situation was now completely stalled, and Roosevelt's proposal of July 24 had become unacceptable for Japan. The Japanese government, which in late July had been occupied with negotiations with the French Vichy government on questions of joint defense and military cooperation, had barely had time to seriously consider Roosevelt's proposal, such was the speed at which the accounts were frozen after the meeting between Roosevelt and Nomura. Washington had put Tokyo under pressure too early, not realizing that Konoe's third cabinet was still in a decisive phase in its foreign policy orientation. The USA had not given the new Japanese government sufficient time to consider the possibility of taking a moderate course of action and of abandoning the former foreign policy, which had been strongly influenced by Matsuoka. In late July, therefore, a great opportunity for rapprochement was wasted. On the contrary, the fronts now appeared to have hardened, and all indications pointed to war.

By now, the Americans were also considering taking not just economic measures, but also other steps against the Japanese Empire. Claire Lee Chennault had long advocated military intervention by the USA on the side of China in the Sino-Japanese conflict. As commander of a squadron of fighter aircraft, he had taken part in maneuvers in the mid-1920s simulating an enemy aerial attack on Pearl Harbor.[55] After Chennault left the US Army Air Corps, forerunner of the US Air Force, he worked as an adviser from 1937 for Chiang Kai-shek's Chinese government. The Chinese sent Chennault to Washington to request volunteers and aircraft to rebuild China's air defense system, which had collapsed during the war with Japan. From summer 1941, he trained the Flying Tigers, a squadron of American volunteers for a combat mission against Japan.

After Japan's intervention in French Indochina, on July 23, 1941, Roosevelt did indeed sign an order authorizing a military operation initiated by Chennault: sixty-six light bombers were to attack Japanese industrial cities so as to hamper the production of arms and goods essential for Japan's economy. The plan was delayed, however, because, among other things, there were not enough planes. In addition, the US political leaders ultimately decided that an oil embargo would be more effective. The idea of a pre-emptive American strike was never implemented and the plan was abandoned. The fact that it was supported at all by Roosevelt and senior admirals Richmond K. Turner and Thomas Hart indicates that America's top politicians and military were visibly frustrated at the aggressive expansionist foreign policy of the Japanese Empire. A diplomatic solution to the American-Japanese conflict was still being sought in summer 1941, but the Americans were now increasingly considering a pre-emptive military strike to settle it.[56]

In Tokyo the intensification of the American embargo policy created great tensions. Politicians and military were split into two camps on the question of war and peace. The rift between doves and hawks was particularly marked in the Japanese navy. On July 31, navy chief-of-staff Admiral Nagano Ōsami had an audience with Emperor Hirohito. Nagano was basically against a war with the USA, but, apparently no longer believing in a negotiated solution, he had already advocated war shortly before the intensification of the American sanctions.[57] He explained to the Emperor: "If the restoration of diplomatic relations with the USA fails, we will no longer receive any oil deliveries, and our reserves will be used up within two years. In the event of war, all oil reserves will be depleted within one and a half years."[58] In reply to a question from the Emperor, Nagano said that there was no guarantee of victory in a long war. The Tripartite Pact was the most disruptive element in American-Japanese relations, but Nagano did not explicitly advocate canceling the alliance with the German Reich, believing that such decisions should be taken by politicians and not the military. Well knowing that the *Nihon Kaigun* was not equipped at the time for a war with the superior US navy, Emperor Hirohito listened impassively to the navy chief-of-staff. No doubt contrary to Nagano's hopes, the Emperor refused to decide one way or another regarding Japan's attitude to the conflict with the USA and was thus of no help in unblocking the situation.[59]

An incident far from Tokyo and Washington inflamed the already heated atmosphere even further. The American gunboat *USS Tutuila* had been stationed in Chungking, China, since the late 1920s and served as an escort ship defending against pirates on the Yangtzekiang. Since the start of the war between China and Japan, however, it had not moved, like all the ships in the Yangtzekiang patrol. After taking Nanking in December 1937 and Wuhan in October 1938, Japanese troops attacked Chungking, the third wartime Chinese capital, in late July 1941. *USS Tutuila* was hit by Japanese bombers in the process on July 31. In response to the US government's vehement protests, the Japanese suspended their bombardment of Chungking for a few days. Relations between the USA and Japan were already strained on account of the French Indochina affair, and the incident made the situation in late July/early August extremely tense. At the same time, Toyoda owed an explanation to Japan's German ally, which had meanwhile become aware of the Japanese exploratory talks and was not at all happy at the news. Toyoda and Nomura reacted immediately to assuage the German Reich. In a telegram on July 31, Nomura informed the German government that the Japanese had delivered a severe blow to the United States through the invasion of French Indochina, which had taken place because of the political encirclement of Japan and the increasing economic constraints. Even if Germany disapproved of the exploratory talks, it could not deny that Japan had deterred the USA from entering the war in Europe.

Japan's actions were thus in complete compliance with the provisions of the Tripartite Pact, Toyoda stressed.[60]

"Our country is at present standing at a most critical crossroads. My only desire is that we choose the right road, for the sake of the future of our country," wrote Nomura on August 7 in a telegram to the *Gaimushō*.[61] In spite of the telegram sent a few days earlier to Berlin (which may be regarded purely as an attempt to reassure its ally), Nomura still hoped that Japan would finally repudiate the Tripartite Pact and that Konoe's third cabinet would decide on a path of reconciliation with Washington. The day before, the Japanese government had presented an alternative to Roosevelt's proposal of July 24. In accordance with the USA's wishes, Japan was willing to withdraw its troops from French Indochina, but only after the termination of the Second Sino-Japanese War, which the Japanese government officially called the "China incident" (*Shina Jihen*). As well as agreeing to general economic cooperation, as a concession Japan also offered to recognize the neutrality of the Philippines, which, according to US plans, would be granted independence after a ten-year transition period and until then was to remain one of the most important US military bases in the Pacific. In response to the Japanese invasion of French Indochina, on July 26 Roosevelt had ordered the defense of the Philippines to be reinforced and had appointed General Douglas MacArthur as commander-in-chief of the US forces in the Far East. The Japanese government also made demands of its own, however. The USA and the Allies should desist from military operations in the south-west Pacific, maintain trade relations and cooperate economically with Japan. Above all, the US government should urge Chiang Kai-shek to end the conflict with Japan.

Hull made clear in his reply that the US government regarded the Japanese proposal as worthless as long as Japan did not abandon its aggressive expansion policy.

To press for an agreement with the USA, on August 7, 1941, Toyoda suggested a personal meeting between Konoe and Roosevelt. He did not expect that the meeting of the heads of government would immediately result in solutions to the issues in dispute, but he believed it would have great symbolic value. The Americans would not consider official negotiations and hence a meeting between Konoe and Roosevelt, however, until Japan ceased its military operations. In talks with Nomura in mid-August, Roosevelt did not mince his words: Japan had ignored his offer of July 24 and had invaded French Indochina instead. Further aggressive and expansionist steps by Japan would force the USA to take measures to protect its own rights and interests. The talks between Hull and Nomura would not be resumed as Japan wished until it ended its policy of expansion. On the contrary, the USA would regard further advances by Japan in south-east Asia as extremely hostile actions, in which case the USA would be forced to defend itself to the limit. "There is only one country that can open the door. This time it's Japan's turn,"[62] Roosevelt told the Japanese government.[63]

In an attempt to keep Japan on the road to peace, Toyoda did indeed do everything possible to arrange a meeting between the two heads of government. Joseph C. Grew, the US ambassador in Tokyo, was impressed by a personal conversation he had with Toyoda on August 16, and by his efforts, but he felt obliged to point out the weakness of the Japanese arguments. While Japan's actions to date had been explained by the fear of encirclement – which Hull had already described to Nomura as "only nonsense"[64] – the invasion of French Indochina was now being justified as a necessary step towards ending the Sino-Japanese War. The official explanation of Japan's foreign policy was thus contradictory, which did nothing to allay American mistrust of Japan's course.

In spite of this, in August 1941 the Japanese government was still hoping for a peaceful settlement of the conflict with the USA. On August 28, Nomura presented his friend Roosevelt with a private message from Konoe, in which he stressed that a personal meeting with the US president was the only way of bringing about a solution to the problems. At a dinner in Tokyo with Grew, Konoe emphasized his desire for peace, while at the same time voices in the media were clamoring for a war with the USA. He stated that because of the unstable political situation in Japan, a meeting with the US president needed to be arranged as soon as possible.

The Japanese prime minister regretted the unfortunate situation in China, although only in private. In public he made no mention either of his country's expansionist course or of the atrocities committed by the army against the Chinese civilian population.[65] It is true that a meeting between Konoe and Roosevelt far from Tokyo would have offered a good opportunity to reach a bilateral agreement without interference by the anti-American hardliners in Japan. Such a meeting would have enabled the Japanese military, the other members of the government, and not least the Emperor himself, to save face, since the outcome, irrespective of the specific content, would have been almost exclusively linked with Konoe himself. For Japan's premier, who was willing in August 1941 to assume this responsibility, the planned meeting would also to some extent have made up for the Japanese expansionist policy hitherto, which he had also been involved in.

The Americans, however, were extremely doubtful that the elegant and worldly Konoe was seriously interested in talks with Roosevelt. The prime minister, who was seen as listless and possessing little political agility, was met with great distrust as a result of his foreign policy, as Hull described in his memoirs: "We could not forget that Konoye had been Premier when

Japan invaded China in 1937; he had signed the Axis
Alliance in 1940 and had concluded the treaty with
the puppet Government in Nanking designated to give
Japan the mastery of China."[66] Other representatives
of US diplomacy, such as Under Secretary Welles, had
faith in Konoe's initiative, but Roosevelt himself was
not convinced by the Japanese proposal. He suspected
that Konoe was motivated not primarily by a genuine
interest in reconciliation with the USA but rather by
the development of the German-Soviet war.[67] Despite
his fundamental suspicions, in public the US president
nevertheless also expressed a willingness to meet Konoe:
"In my opinion, the President is the one who shows
the most interest in the 'leader's conference,'"[68] wrote
Nomura in a telegram to Tokyo. The Japanese suggested Hawaii as the venue for a meeting in the near
future. Roosevelt preferred Juneau, Alaska. In his reply
to Konoe's personal message, the president stressed that
fundamental principles would have to be agreed before-
hand and that only then could official talks take place.
He was referring to the four Basic Principles formulated
in mid-April 1941 by the Americans (respect for the
territorial integrity and sovereignty of all states, non-
interference in the internal affairs of other countries,
equality – above all in trade – for all countries, and no
change in the status quo in the Pacific through military
actions).

Instead of responding to these demands, Japan sent a
further proposal to Washington. It would not advance
further in south-east Asia unless warranted, for example by further economic sanctions by the USA against
Japan. If, by contrast, the USA were to enter the war
in Europe, Japan would have to act in accordance
with its own interpretation of the provisions of the
Tripartite Pact. On conclusion of an agreement with the
Chinese government, Japan would withdraw its troops
from China. It would cooperate with the USA in trade

relations. Nomura described this as the "maximum limit to which our government could go."[69] Toyoda was optimistic that the US government would respect the Japanese concessions and unfreeze the assets. Hull was reticent about the new Japanese proposal, not least because he was no doubt unsure of the stability of the inexperienced government in Tokyo. Nomura thought that the Americans were playing for time and hoped that the continuing economic pressure by the USA would make the Japanese see reason and accept the American four Basic Principles. At the same time, he reckoned, Roosevelt feared that Konoe's cabinet would collapse and for that reason did not want to press the Japanese government too hard. Following an agreement between Japan and the USA, the US Pacific Fleet could be transferred to the Atlantic and intervene in the war in Europe, something that Churchill in particular was hoping for.

Meanwhile, the opinion prevailed in Tokyo in early September 1941 that the military conquest of south-east Asia was the only way for Japan to gain access to the natural resources that it considered vital for the war effort and that it was lacking owing to the US embargo since July. Japan's oil reserves would allow it to continue the war with China only for a maximum of two years. For the military elite, the resolution of the conflict desired by the USA – withdrawal of the Japanese troops from French Indochina and a ceasefire in China – was not a political option but a humiliation. By the end of August the army and navy general staffs had come to the conclusion that a military confrontation with the Western powers was inevitable if the Japanese diplomats could not reach an acceptable agreement with the USA. Discussion now hinged solely on how long Japan should continue to confine itself to diplomacy to achieve an agreement. At the imperial conference on September 6, Japan's political and military leaders formulated some "guidelines for implementing imperial national policy" (*teikoku kokusaku suikō yōryō*).[70] In line with the Japanese concept of establishing a "Greater Asia Co-Prosperity Sphere" – a block of Asian nations independent of Western colonialism and led by Japan, living at peace and prospering together – the influence of the West in Asia needed to end and resources had to be acquired to wage a drawn-out war with the USA. Navy chief-of-staff Admiral Nagano was of the opinion that Japan would be able to wage a long war of attrition if it conquered the most important areas of south-east Asia and the western Pacific at the outset of the conflict. But the navy representatives were still reluctant to engage in a direct confrontation with the US navy and therefore suggested that a solution through diplomacy be further pursued. By contrast, representatives of the army, led by chief-of-staff Field Marshal Sugiyama Hajime, were in favor of going to war as soon as possible before the Allies were ready and equipped and no longer capable of being defeated. The army and navy ultimately reached a compromise to complete war preparations by the end of October and then to discuss the issue of war again. If war were then favored, Japan would be ready to conduct military operations immediately. Parallel to the war preparations, however, diplomatic channels should be used intensively. The guidelines clearly outlined both Japan's minimum requirements and its maximum concessions. The USA and Great Britain should not interfere in the Sino-Japanese conflict and should cease to support Chiang Kai-shek. Peace with China should be agreed purely on Japanese terms. International trade relations were to be resumed and Japan granted access to vital natural resources in Asia. In return, Japan promised not to advance from its "base in Indochina" to neighboring territories. China was explicitly excluded from this concession. In the event that peace were restored in Asia, Japan could conceive

withdrawing its troops from French Indochina some-
time in the future.

If, after October 10, a negotiated solution and the
meeting of the Japanese demands appeared impossible, "a decision should be adopted without delay to
declare war on the USA (as well as England and the
Netherlands)." A war on two fronts against the Soviet
Union and the USA should be avoided at all costs. In
view of the fact that Japan had already missed an oppor-
tune moment to attack the Soviet Union in the summer
– directly after the start of Operation Barbarossa – in
September Japan's war strategists effectively identified
the USA as their future adversary, and the imperial conference basically approved the declaration of war.

Toyoda, who assumed that the desired meeting
between Konoe and Roosevelt would take place soon,
remained optimistic in the first half of September, as
did Nomura, not least as the Americans had presented
a new proposal on September 10. Both Nomura and his
counterpart Hull believed that the latest proposals by
both countries had more points in common than previous ones. The Japanese ambassador was convinced that
texts relating to the points that had been discussed for
weeks were now formulated in such a way that agreement could be reached without further ado. In his view,
the USA and Japan had finally come a step closer after
weeks of prevarication. The "China question" remained
a sticking point, however. The USA indicated that it
would make no contribution to resolving the China
problem as long as Japan did not agree to the four Basic
Principles, a troop withdrawal, and the equality principle in trade on the Chinese market. Regarding China,
the Americans interpreted the proposal submitted by
Japan as a clear restriction on US policy in the Pacific.
Nomura now felt that his own government should act
and requested that it conclude the following agreement
with the USA: Japan would withdraw its troops from

China within two years after the restoration of peace. This would give it some leeway in the short term while still leaving the option, should the situation change, of concluding an agreement in the future to enable Japanese garrisons to remain longer.

On September 22, 1941, Toyoda explained Japan's China policy to US ambassador Grew. It entailed recognition of the territorial integrity and sovereignty of China. The Chinese and Japanese units stationed in China should form a bulwark against communism. Finally, China and Japan should enter into a trade cooperation. A basic prerequisite for this was China's recognition of Manchukuo and the formation of a new Chinese government combining Chiang Kai-shek's government with the Chinese government put in place by the Japanese in Nanking. A declaration would guarantee that there would be no further annexations or demands for compensation. The Japanese were aware of Roosevelt's wish to conclude an agreement of principle as a basis for the talks before the meeting of the two heads of government, but Toyoda believed that the details could be discussed and dealt with at the meeting, which was planned for mid-October – the first, incidentally, by a Japanese head of government outside his own country. No time should be lost, the foreign minister reckoned, since the mood in the country was moving increasingly towards the Axis, and the first anniversary of the signing of the Tripartite Pact could be exploited for propaganda purposes by anti-American forces in Japan. US ambassador Grew had also noted the increasingly strident public demand not to agree to the withdrawal of troops from Indochina and, in particular, China. As he believed that a further weakening of Japan's economy and foreign policy would be of benefit to the communist Soviet Union – which he saw as the greatest threat to world peace – he advised his own government against continuing to put economic

pressure on Japan and to continue working construc-
tively towards a diplomatic solution.

Behind the scenes, Japan's military preparations were
steaming ahead. The commander of the Combined
Fleet (rengō kantai shirei chōkan), Admiral Yamamoto
Isoroku, was put in charge of planning a surprise
attack on Pearl Harbor. In late September, he informed
Admiral Nagano that the preparations for war would
be completed by mid-November. They included the
advance on a wide front in south-east Asia and the
south Pacific, with attacks on the US bases in Pearl
Harbor and the Philippines, and the British stronghold
of Singapore. Yamamoto calculated that the Japanese
campaign would take four months to reach a successful conclusion. As to the longer-term prospects, he was
much more cautious. It could be assumed that the war
with the USA would be a long one and that, in spite of
potential military defeats in the early stages, its adversary would not give up, banking rather on its superior
economic power. Yamamoto doubted that Japan could
match the US war industry. He also reckoned that there
would be shortages of natural resources. He had told
Konoe shortly before that the navy could only fight for
one and a half years at the most and that he could not
predict how the war would go thereafter. "A war with
such small prospects for success should not be waged,"
his counterpart Nagano concluded.[71] Like the navy vet-
erans Toyoda and Nomura, Yamamoto wanted to avoid
a Japanese-American war in the Pacific at all costs.

On September 25, a liaison conference[72] attended
by the prime minister, the ministers of the army, navy,
foreign affairs and finance as representatives of the
government, and the chiefs of the general staff of the
army and navy as spokespersons for the military, determined that an agreement had to be reached with the
USA by October 15, otherwise Japan would break off
the talks with the US. As at the imperial conference on

September 6, the end of October was envisaged for the start of the attack. Sugiyama, the army chief-of-staff, stressed that it would not be sufficient for the negotiations with the USA to result in a short-term peace arrangement of just a few years. Japan could accept only a long-term agreement that would guarantee peace for decades. If this could not be achieved, the bilateral talks should be discontinued on October 15. As the liaison conference unanimously backed the attitude of the army formulated by Sugiyama, a time limit was now set on a diplomatic solution. The negotiators in Washington therefore had only a few days to prevent the outbreak of a major conflict in the Pacific. Japan was heading for war with ominous speed – a prospect that Konoe could only contemplate with increasing resignation. As he confessed to his friend Lord Keeper of the Privy Seal Kido, he no longer felt able to deal with this national crisis and was thinking of stepping down from office.[73]

On October 2, the US government communicated to Tokyo its official reply to the Japanese proposal from September. The text and, particularly, its similarity with the text of the very first Japanese proposals, made it unacceptable. "It is the President's earnest hope that discussion of the fundamental questions may be so developed that such a meeting can be held,"[74] said Hull to Nomura. Roosevelt was still not averse to meeting Konoe but continued to demand Japan's agreement to the Principles formulated by the USA.

The two countries remained in fundamental disagreement on three points: the basic structure of the economic relations in the Pacific, Japan's troop withdrawal, and the interpretation of the Tripartite Pact – in particular, for the Americans, how Japan would react to a possible involvement by the USA in the war in Europe. Neither the USA nor Japan was willing to budge from its position, and so in early October 1941 the situation was completely deadlocked. Nomura, who also regarded the proposal submitted by Japan in early September as too inflexible, now suggested to his government that it accept the four Basic Principles postulated by the USA after all. He believed that their formulation was vague enough to allow room for interpretation. In a telegram to the *Gaimushō* he stated quite clearly: "I am sure that there is not the slightest chance on earth of them featuring a conference of leaders so long as we do not make that compromise."[75]

On October 9, Konoe met Lord Keeper of the Privy Seal Kido after he had informed the Emperor of the status of the talks in Washington and the growing danger of war. His old friend urged the prime minister – who had been the object of an assassination attempt the previous month by warmongering ultra-nationalists, and who was increasingly concerned by the strident demands for his resignation – not to lose faith in a peaceful solution. The decision by the imperial conference on September 6 had been hasty and not well thought out. Japan's chances of winning a war against the USA were small, as the groundwork for victory had not yet been laid. For that reason the Japanese government should not under any circumstances decide to declare war but should rather focus on ending the hostilities with China.[76] Encouraged by Kido, Konoe undertook one last attempt to resolve the tensions between Japan and the USA by peaceful means.

On October 12, he invited foreign minister Toyoda, navy minister Oikawa, army minister Tōjō, and the director of the planning office Suzuki to his home. As Japan was in the midst of a serious foreign policy crisis, there was no time to celebrate Konoe's fiftieth birthday. The prime minister wanted to make one last attempt to avert war. There were only a few hours until October 15, the deadline the Japanese government itself had set for a diplomatic agreement with the USA. As yet, no agreement was in sight. While army minister Tōjō insisted fervently on breaking off bilateral negotiations, referring to the recent decision in favor of war, Konoe was adamant in his support of a negotiated solution, stressing that no one could predict how long a war with the USA would last. Navy minister Oikawa demanded that Konoe show his strong leadership and make his position clear but made no attempt himself to oppose the warmongering Tōjō. In doing so he missed the opportunity of making it absolutely clear how ill-prepared the navy was to wage war against the USA.

Oikawa personally wished for a continuation of the confidential talks in Washington but preferred to leave it to Konoe to decide on war or peace – true to the belief that politicians determine the course and the military follows.[77] As a military man, he believed that politicians rather than the military should assume the responsibility in such matters. He was also aware that the navy was divided on the question of war and peace with the USA. The leading figures in the ministry of the navy and the commander of the Combined Fleet Admiral Yamamoto were in favor of a diplomatic solution, while the admiralty preferred war. In the middle ranks of the navy the mood was also shifting towards war.[78] A clear vote from him in favor of peace and against war would cause great conflict within the navy, the minister feared. For prestige reasons as well, Oikawa was reluctant to acknowledge that the *Nihon Kaigun* was not ready for war. He did not want to show any sign of weakness to Tōjō and the army as a whole, with which a traditional rivalry had existed for decades. In retrospect, a clear opposition to war would have been a demonstrative sign of strength that might possibly even have quieted the warmongering voices in the army.

Like so many other members of the Japanese military, Tōjō also thought in purely military categories. His soldierly habits would not allow him to accept even a partial withdrawal from China, which would represent for him a shameful defeat: "We have already sacrificed thousands of lives during the China incident. A withdrawal of the troops [from China] is therefore an untenable option."[79] The lives of thousands of Japanese soldiers were not to have been sacrificed in vain. For that reason alone, there was no question for him of accepting the Americans' Basic Principles.

For the time being, however, Tōjō kept his personal opinion to himself. In his function as minister of the army and hence the most important representative of the land forces, he was the spokesman for the army, in which the radical warmongering faction now had the upper hand. At the same time, he belonged to the group within the army that would oppose the war in the event that the navy was not ready for combat. For that reason as well, he was waiting for the minister of the navy to take a clear stance – for peace and against the war. By refusing to state categorically that a war was impossible, however, the navy minister shifted responsibility for the decision onto the prime minister and his government. As a military man, Oikawa did not consider it his task to interfere in politics.

The meeting at Konoe's house once again revealed that Japan's political and military leadership was in a serious crisis with regard to the question of war. A unanimous decision was not in sight. Within the cabinet, Konoe and Toyoda were still convinced that a breakthrough could be achieved by diplomatic means, although Japan would have to make concessions on troop withdrawals. Tōjō was in favor of abiding by the decision of September 6. The army categorically excluded the possibility of a troop withdrawal from China or Indochina, while Oikawa remained noticeably reticent on account of the discord within the navy.

As the fronts were so hardened and the self-imposed deadline was about to expire, the formation of a new cabinet appeared to be the only way to maintain Japan's political viability. In this political constellation and without a clear stance on the part of the navy, the government's hands were tied. A person had to be sought who was capable of coordinating the army and navy policies. This situation demonstrated how much the two services, fierce rivals in other respects as well, tended to pursue their own political agendas, which represented a considerable structural problem for Japan. Numerous politicians, including the weary Konoe himself, were in favor of turning to a member of the imperial family to solve the problem. Hirohito's uncle, Prince Higashikuni, "a declared opponent of war,"[80] now came into consideration as Konoe's successor as prime minister. The court was hesitant about such a move, however. Lord Keeper of the Privy Seal Kido was against the idea of placing the imperial family at the forefront of political decision-making, especially in the absence of consensus between the army and navy. He was concerned that the imperial household would be exposed to public criticism if a cabinet led by Higashikuni failed to solve the problem and a war were to break out with the USA. Instead, Kido urged that the hasty decision of September 6 be reviewed and that agreement on a basic political course be achieved between the army and navy. In autumn 1941, therefore, the Japanese imperial household was also reluctant to take responsibility for the critical domestic and foreign policy situation.[81]

Until then, only a few of those involved had recognized the basic problem of Japanese-American relations that had brought the diplomatic process to a standstill. Among them was Wakasugi Kaname, a member of the embassy staff, who summed up the situation in a conversation with Sumner Welles, US Under Secretary of State, on October 13, 1941.[82] While the Americans were mainly quibbling about the acceptance by Japan of the wide-ranging Basic Principles – the macro level, as it were – Japan from the outset had concentrated on questions of detail and specific assurance – the micro

level. Unlike the government in Tokyo, the USA with its
four Basic Principles was pursuing an aim of sustainable
peace in the Pacific and was thus adopting a long-term
perspective. Cordell Hull wrote in his memoirs after
the war: "On our part we had been truly anxious to
reach an agreement that would make peace in the
Pacific possible, not for a few months but for years or
generations."[83] By contrast, Japan, bogged down in
the conflict in China, sought a meeting between Konoe
and Roosevelt in order to find a short-term solution
to the problem. However, American supporters of the
meeting, such as US ambassador Grew, were unable to
convince their own government of the significance of a
personal encounter between the two heads of government. For their part, those in Japan who wanted peace
with the USA, led by Nomura, Toyoda, and Konoe himself, placed all of their hopes in such a meeting.[84]

The US government as a whole had little understanding of Japan's proposals, which were aimed at short-term
solutions. It insisted on prior recognition of its four
Principles. Although it never made an official announce-
ment to that effect, this insistence effectively signified a
rejection of a meeting between the two heads of government. Neither the Japanese nor the American negotiators
recognized the fundamental misunderstanding, in retrospect so clearly evident from the various proposals
submitted by either side. For weeks, the diplomatic
representatives of the two countries had to a certain
extent been talking at cross purposes. For months, representatives of the US government and Konoe's cabinet
had held dozens of talks, sent countless telegrams, and
drafted several guideline papers without achieving any
significant rapprochement between the parties. They had
both stubbornly held to their own points of view and
with their uncompromising attitudes basically brought
about a diplomatic stalemate, which was to have far-
reaching consequences for the Japanese Empire and the

course of World War II. As Konoe wrote to Nomura in a telegram on October 17, the wholesale resignation of his cabinet the previous day had ultimately been due to the discord within his government regarding the withdrawal of troops from China. The prime minister had not been persuasive enough to change Japan's policy. He had not been able to wring concessions from Tōjō and the army in the matter, but without such a compromise, a diplomatic solution with the USA was completely impossible.

Japan's proposals for resolving the conflict

After the resignation of Konoe's cabinet and the refusal of the imperial household to step in, the only way for the urgently required agreement between the army and navy to be achieved was to appoint a member of the military as the new prime minister. Supporters of a moderate approach suggested the retired general Ugaki Kazushige, who had already been proposed for this office in 1937 but had not been able to obtain the necessary support from the army. In autumn 1941 he was still a controversial figure within the army. He was unfamiliar with the domestic and foreign policy developments of the previous years – unlike Tōjō and Oikawa, ministers of the army and navy, respectively, who were now also under discussion as potential candidates for the office of prime minister. As they had been involved in the decision of September 6, they were both considered capable of overcoming the indecisiveness, of aligning the army and the navy, and of carefully reviewing and if necessary rescinding the war decision. The choice was ultimately made in favor of Tōjō, who had been proposed by Lord Keeper of the Privy Seal Kido. He was believed to have a better overview of the military as a whole and of the army in particular, and would also have the backing of the army.[85] As required by the Constitution, he was

appointed prime minister by the Emperor. Tōjō had
supported the candidacy of Prince Higashikuni and
had not sought the office himself. He was known to be
an opponent of Russia and was in close contact with
the Kwantung army stationed in China, whose leadership had been eager to attack the Soviet Union ever
since Barbarossa. For a short time at least after Tōjō's
appointment, the rumor therefore spread in Tokyo that
war with the Soviet Union was imminent.[86] To allay
fears in Washington, Konoe had contacted Grew in the
hour of his resignation[87] and asked him to do everything
he could for peace, even if the new government under
Tōjō, who as minister of the army had voted for war,
appeared more radical.

"I cannot tell you how much in the dark I am,"[88]
wrote an evidently frustrated ambassador Nomura in
Washington to the new prime minister. The months
of unsuccessful discussion had worn him out. In the
telegram he criticized in particular the lack of communication between the *Gaimushō* and the navy. Nomura
let it be known that he was at the end of his tether: "I
don't want to be the bones of a dead horse. I don't want
to continue this hypocritical existence, deceiving other
people. No, don't think I am trying to flee from the field
of battle, but as a man of honor this is the only way that
is open for me to tread. Please send me your permission
to return to Japan."[89] His wish to follow Konoe and
Toyoda seemed only logical. With them he had tried
in vain to maintain a *modus vivendi* with the USA and
had failed because of the "China question." The answer
from Tokyo came without delay: the new government
denied the request, since the ambassador's peace mission was still not ended.

Meanwhile, the personnel changes continued in
Tokyo. The minister of the navy in the new cabinet
led by Tōjō was Shimada Shigetarō, who had studied
at the naval academy alongside Yamamoto. Shimada

was soon being described as Tōjō's lackey. Replacing the moderate Toyoda as minister for foreign affairs was Tōgō Shigenori. After World War I, Tōgō had been a member of the diplomatic service posted to Berlin during the Weimar Republic. There he had met Edith de Lalande, the widow of a Prussian government architect, whom he had married following his return to Japan in 1922. He had a weakness for German culture in general and German literature in particular, and since his days in Berlin at the latest he had felt a strong personal attachment to the German Reich. He traveled frequently to Germany during the 1930s and in 1937/8 was even ambassador there for a short while. He was not a forthright supporter of the Nazis, however, and had also worked in the mid-1920s in the embassy in Washington. Nonetheless, the Americans took his appointment as foreign minister in October 1941 as a sign that the *Gaimushō* was now more interested in maintaining good relations with the German Reich than in reaching a compromise with the USA. Tōgō was also seen as a friend of the Soviet Union, another ideological enemy of the USA.

As soon as he took office, the new Japanese foreign minister faced a gargantuan task. Given the lack of success of the negotiations to date, he believed that it would be difficult to get Washington to adopt a more accommodating attitude to Japan. The Japanese had seen no indications that the USA would change its course, and Tōgō had not noticed any willingness to compromise in Japan either. Konoe's cabinet had failed because of disagreements on the "China question," and the army had supported the continued stationing of troops in China – a position that Prime Minister Konoe had ultimately felt unable to endorse. Tōgō knew that he too would have to persuade the army representatives to agree to concessions. He also had to bear the consequences of the mid-October deadline set in early September, which had been put back to November 15 on account of the formation of the new government. Tōgō took office in an atmosphere of pessimism – he rightly saw that there was little prospect of a peaceful solution being achieved with the USA quite literally at the eleventh hour.[90]

In late October 1941, Tōjō's government agreed with the USA that both sides should draft new proposals for discussion. Japan's representatives were hoping for an agreement with the USA by November 15, the day on which the Japanese parliament in Tokyo would be officially convened. US ambassador Grew was reporting to Washington that Japan's military leaders were against a peaceful settlement of the conflict with the USA. The Emperor himself, who was very pro-American, had ordered the military to obey him, however, resulting in the appointment of Tōjō, a man capable of controlling the military, as prime minister. Grew's hopes for peace therefore rested on Emperor Hirohito, who, as a presumed supporter of a peaceful solution, could exert a suitable influence on the new cabinet. The US ambassador was not aware, however, that in difficult situations the Emperor was neither a strong personality nor a man of resolute words and decisions.[91]

In fact, by the time Tōjō's government had formed at the latest, the military had taken control of the Japanese state, something that also became clear to Tōgō when he was appointed foreign minister in October 1941. He was surprised to discover that Japan's military authorities were informed unilaterally of all diplomatic correspondence and hence all of the *Gaimushō*'s written messages concerning the ongoing Japanese-American negotiations. Japanese diplomacy was now influenced and monitored by the military.

On November 3, Grew was informed in Tokyo that Japan's prime minister, navy minister, and foreign minister had reached an agreement on the maximum extent of Japanese concessions, which was now to be submitted to the Emperor. Grew emphasized to the State Department that in Japan's view the war with China could not be dissociated from the war in Europe. Japan should not be driven into a corner through further economic sanctions, as this could result in the severing of diplomatic relations. But Grew was also unwilling to make further concessions to Japan. He reported to Washington that the warmongering voices in the Japanese media were becoming increasingly strident and that the USA should continue to insist on the Basic Principles. He also expressed his fear that the Japanese government could take steps that would make war with the USA inevitable. He could not yet foresee in early November 1941 how near to the truth his suspicions were.[92]

Just two days later, on November 5, 1941, Admiral Yamamoto issued the strictly confidential order number 1 to his fleet on preparations for an attack on the US naval base in Pearl Harbor.[93] If no peaceful agreement with Washington was achieved, Japan's attack would take place on December 7, 1941, Hawaiian time/ December 8 Japanese time. Nomura had had good reason to complain so emphatically in his resignation speech about the lack of coordination between the navy and Japanese diplomats. He was as unaware as his interlocutors in the American capital that Yamamoto was hatching war plans at the same time as Nomura was endeavoring to negotiate a peaceful solution.

In the meantime, the government ministers had held several liaison meetings from October 23 to 30 with the chiefs of the army and navy general staffs. They quickly came to the conclusion that diplomacy had reached its limits: a diplomatic solution was still not in sight, and war should therefore be declared without delay. The plan was to reopen diplomatic negotiations with Washington shortly after the outbreak of war and the initial military successes of the navy, which Admiral Nagano gave firm assurances of, so as to achieve a negotiated peace. It was clearly pointed out at the meetings that Japan would not have sufficient resources to wage a drawn-out conflict. The military authorities omitted to point out more explicitly, however, that a protracted war would be in the interests of Washington, which was economically superior. Nor did the participants at the meeting take into account that in the event of a war in the Pacific the USA would not be willing to negotiate but would prove as determined as Great Britain was in its war against the German Reich. They merely confirmed the foreign policy principle, formulated at the imperial conferences in the summer, of not recoiling at the prospect of war. The discussion in late October 1941 in Tokyo therefore no longer focused on a basic decision between war and peace but only on the most favorable time for what was now seen as an inevitable opening of hostilities – without discussing an official declaration of war according to international law. In view of the war in Europe, it was debated whether to postpone the outbreak of hostilities until the end of March 1942. However, because of the dwindling Japanese oil reserves – a direct result of the US embargo – the general staff was keen on starting as soon as possible. The idea of a postponement was therefore soon discarded by Tōjō, whose opinion carried most weight in the liaison conferences. After finance minister Kaya had once again drawn attention at the conference on October 30 to the supply problems faced by Japan, foreign minister Tōgō also advocated a peaceful solution and emphasized: "Our economy will survive even if we agree to a troop withdrawal. The sooner it is done, the better."[94] Even he had to concede, however, that Japan would be making a great sacrifice were it to withdraw extensively from China and French Indochina.

Ultimately, the politicians and military representatives agreed to offer to withdraw the troops from northern China, Inner Mongolia, and the island of Hainan within twenty-five years, should the Americans insist on a fixed deadline. Withdrawal from French Indochina would take place only after the war with China had been ended peacefully. Adhesion to the Tripartite Pact was confirmed. And so as not to completely reject the four Basic Principles, they would agree to the principle of free trade in the world and hence also in China. A letter designated "Plan A" was drafted with this text and sent to the Japanese embassy in Washington. At a further liaison conference on November 1, however, it was clearly stated that apart from the presentation of this last diplomatic offer to Washington, war preparations were to be continued. Arguing that an attack would give Japan control of the natural resources of south-east Asia, Admiral Nagano once again urged that the war start as soon as possible. This would be greatly advantageous for Japan and "better than waiting another three years,"[95] as this would give the USA time to prepare for war much better than Japan. In the seventeen-hour meeting it was ultimately decided to give diplomacy one last chance until midnight on December 1. If agreement was still not reached by then, Japan would open hostilities.

The liaison conferences had made clear that Japan was ready for confrontation if the USA could not be moved to relent by way of diplomacy. Japan's new government would not consider simply accepting the four Basic Principles. It believed that it had already made sufficient concessions and was now heading for war with the USA. Foreign minister Tōgō also realized this, convinced as he was that the Americans would not accept the Japanese Plan A. As a further final peace option, Tōgō sent ambassador Nomura a "Plan B" offering as a basis for negotiation the renunciation of military advances in south-east Asia by both Japan and the USA. The USA would also supply Japan with oil and lift the freezing order imposed in July, and the countries would cooperate economically with regard to the oil reserves in Dutch East India. Japan also offered to withdraw its troops from the south of French Indochina to the north. A full withdrawal from the peninsula would occur whenever peace with China or a general peaceful solution in the Pacific was achieved. At the insistence of the army representatives, chief-of-staff Sugiyama and his deputy Tsukada, however, Plan B contained a further clause forbidding the USA from intervening in a peace process between Japan and China. This once again indicated the maximum extent of concessions Japan was willing to allow and represented a further attempt at negotiation under the terms that had prevailed before July 1941 – in other words, before the Japanese invasion of French Indochina and the intensification of the US embargo.

At the imperial conference on November 5, the Emperor also endorsed the decisions to reach agreement with the USA through diplomatic channels by submitting Plans A and B. Otherwise hostilities would commence in early December. A deadline was thus set by Japan for a diplomatic solution. Only a few days remained to avert a war, which the Japanese military was also preparing for at the same time.

The very same day, the *Gaimushō* transmitted Plans A and B to Nomura with the instruction to achieve an agreement with the USA on this basis by November 25. The ambassador was completely unaware that the political and military decision-makers in Tokyo had in reality set the date for an attack on Pearl Harbor in early December in the event that no agreement could be reached. Nomura handed over Plan A to Hull on November 7, 1941. Hull expressed satisfaction at the formulations for agreeing the principle of economic equality, but was less satisfied with the idea of just a partial Japanese troop withdrawal. He also asked whether Japan would be interested in a meeting of Japanese and Chinese leaders mediated by the USA, which had been explicitly ruled out through the clause included in Plan B at the insistence of the army representatives. Tōgō, who had reluctantly given in to the vehement insistence of the army representatives and included the clause in Plan B, appeared pleased at Hull's suggestion of a meeting between Japan and China. At the same time, he hoped that the USA would ultimately leave it to those two countries to find a peaceful solution. Even if his own attitude in this regard might have been different, Japan's foreign minister, following the official Japanese line, first demanded a guarantee from the USA that it would cease its aid to Chiang Kai-shek and not interfere in Sino-Japanese negotiations.[96]

At a meeting in Tokyo on November 10, 1941 – just a few hours after Nomura had met Hull – convened by the Japanese to emphasize the urgency of the situation, foreign minister Tōgō informed US ambassador Grew that the shortage of natural resources was becoming critical for Japan and that an agreement had to be reached urgently before November 15, the day on which the Japanese parliament reconvened. Pointing out that Japan had made a number of concessions regarding economic equality in the Pacific and the stationing of troops in China, Tōgō also presented Plan A, stating that it was "the maximum compromise that we can endure to make."[97] The core point was the critical question of the presence of Japanese troops in China. Tōgō stressed: "Furthermore, insofar as the China question is concerned, would you have us ignore the successes gained as a result of sacrifices that we have made over four and a half years? Submission to terms such as these [demanded previously by the USA] would be suicidal for Japan. For the government, as well as for the people, I believe that such a course is impossible."[98]

Even though the US negotiators were happy with many of the proposals in Plan A – such as the trade cooperation – the bilateral discussions were tough. While the USA still found Japan's continued adherence to the Tripartite Pact to be a problem, the Japanese diplomats could not obtain an agreement from the USA to stay out of the China peace negotiations. Moreover, Roosevelt demanded from his friend Nomura a guarantee that Japan would desist from further aggression in the Far East, stressing that for a mutually satisfactory agreement to be reached, "it is necessary to find a *modus vivendi.*"[99] He did not elaborate on the kind of *modus vivendi* he envisaged. Nomura interpreted it as a "provisional agreement."[100]

In a meeting with Nomura on November 15 in reaction to the Japanese Plan A, Hull confirmed the internationally valid economic equality accepted by the Japanese government: Japan should be able to act in the economic sphere in partnership with the USA under the principle of free trade. This conversation made it quite clear, however, that the two sides had a different interpretation of the nature of their consultations. Because the decision to go to war had already been made in Japan, time was running out for its diplomats, who saw the talks as the last chance of ensuring peace. If the US government found the proposals made by Tōjō's government to be unacceptable, they hoped at least to be able to make counter-proposals. The US negotiators were not under any time pressure and believed that time was on their side. Sooner or later, Japan would relent in the meetings, which the Americans continued to regard as exploratory talks. In response to Nomura's question regarding the US position on the unresolved questions of the Tripartite Pact and the Japanese troops stationed in China, Hull replied that his government would first have to consult with Great Britain, China, and the Netherlands. Moreover, official peace negotiations could not start until Japan renounced the Tripartite Pact. As long as it adhered to it, the American public would not accept a peace treaty with Japan. Nomura now felt his suspicions confirmed, as he had stated in a confidential message to his government the previous day: the United States was establishing ever-closer ties with China and assisting Chiang Kai-shek as far as possible, and would not therefore favor Japan at China's expense. It would not accept the Japanese proposal as it stood, because it wanted to avoid another Munich agreement and had finally abandoned the policy of appeasement practiced towards Hitler. On the contrary, it was now ready to take up arms to prevent further expansion by Japan.[101]

On the same day, November 15, 1941, an envoy from the *Gaimushō* arrived in Washington hoping to give last-ditch momentum to the bilateral talks. Officially, Japan's special envoy Kurusu Saburō had been sent to the US capital once again to stress the urgency for the Japanese government of the current round of talks and to assist Nomura, whose English was known to be deficient. A further reason for engaging Kurusu was that Tōgō did not think much of his ambassador in Washington. For his part, Nomura had asked Tōgō's predecessor for support, explicitly mentioning "a man like Kurusu,"[102] who understood the game of diplomacy but was also familiar with internal Japanese politics. Kurusu was married to an American and had known Cordell Hull, who was from Tennessee, for a long time, having discussed trade matters with him while head of the *Gaimushō* commercial department before becoming ambassador to Belgium in 1936.[103] And yet the appointment of Kurusu as special envoy was not a fortunate one on this occasion: he was not a supporter of the Nazis but, as ambassador in Berlin, he had signed the Tripartite Pact in 1940 and was to be seen in numerous photos at Hitler's side.[104] A few days before his arrival in Washington, during a stopover in Manila, a correspondent of *The New York Times* had drawn the pessimistic comment from him that "there was 'not much hope' that his dramatic flying trip to Washington would be successful."[105] From the outset, therefore, Kurusu's mission as special envoy was under a bad sign and seen in Washington as problematic.

At first, however, Kurusu appeared to bring fresh impetus to the Washington talks. When he met Hull and then Roosevelt on the morning of November 17, the cheerful and friendly president seemed interested in peace and willing to negotiate. Roosevelt emphasized that the USA did not wish to intervene in Sino-Japanese relations but to function as an "introducer." Compared to the president, Hull appeared much more resolute, pointing to the American interpretation of its right to self-defense. The US government could not afford to wait for the German Reich to conquer England and then attack the USA with the British fleet. Roosevelt skillfully steered the conversation to the historical friendship between the two countries, repeating the comment by Secretary of State William Jennings Bryan to the Japanese ambassador Chinda Sutemi a quarter of a century earlier: "There is no last word between friends."[106] Japan's diplomats understood this to mean that the US government would try everything to keep the peace, once again reinforcing the hope of a diplomatic solution. One of the participants was less optimistic, however. From the outset, Hull was highly distrustful of Kurusu, not least because he had personally signed the Tripartite Pact. No doubt to sound the envoy out on this matter, Hull first brought up not the "China question" but the Tripartite Pact.[107] While Hull demanded that the alliance be dissolved, Kurusu defended the treaty. It had been concluded, he said, to prevent war in future and "in fact to keep peace."[108] In view of these divergent interpretations, the fronts quickly hardened again.

In order nevertheless to seek a solution to the "China question," Kurusu suggested the following deal: would it not be possible, in return for the withdrawal of Japanese troops from French Indochina, for the USA to ease the economic sanctions and send at least a small amount of rice and oil to Japan? The government would then guarantee that these supplies were for the civilian population of Japan rather than the military.[109] Following up this first proposal, the USA might consider unfreezing Japanese assets in return for the withdrawal of Japanese troops from the south of French Indochina, since it was the occupation of this territory a few months before that had prompted the USA to impose such drastic economic sanctions. As Hull also agreed that a gesture of this nature could indeed calm Japanese public opinion, the end of the diplomatic ill feeling appeared to be within grasp.

When Tōgō was informed of the results of the talks in Washington, however, he was furious. Without the authorization of the *Gaimushō*, and although Japan had not yet received an official reply from the USA on Plan A, Nomura and Kurusu had overreached themselves in the bilateral talks. By proposing the withdrawal of troops from the south of French Indochina, they had prematurely revealed an essential component of Plan B. The two Japanese diplomats had not consulted sufficiently with the foreign ministry in Tokyo and, focusing on the deadline set by the *Gaimushō*, had been guided by the time pressure and their interest in bringing the talks to a rapid conclusion. In doing so, they had undermined Tōgō's aim of somehow having Plan A accepted.[110]

In this situation, Japan had no choice now but to officially offer the US government its Plan B, its *ultima ratio*. Nomura handed Hull Japan's final proposal on Thanksgiving Day 1941 (November 20).[111] Japan would withdraw its troops from the south to the north of French Indochina if the USA unfroze Japanese assets, resumed trade relations, provided Japan with the oil it needed, and refrained from any actions that could jeopardize the restoration of peace between China and

Japan. Hull promised to study the new proposal in detail but emphasized in his immediate reaction that, like Great Britain, the USA could not refuse to help China as long as Japan did not demonstrate its peaceful intentions by withdrawing from the Tripartite Pact. At first glance, Japan's most recent proposal appeared to be equivalent to a "surrender"[112] by the USA and was thus absolutely unacceptable.

On November 22, Nomura informed Hull that he had also conferred with representatives of other governments in Washington – namely the ambassadors of China, Great Britain, and the Dutch government in exile. They all confirmed that no satisfactory compromise was possible with Japan as long as it failed to demonstrate its peaceful intentions. The Japanese troops stationed in French Indochina represented a threat to neighboring countries and called for military remedies. The withdrawal of troops from the south to the north of French Indochina was not a satisfactory solution. Nomura replied that Japan required troops in the north of French Indochina in order to maintain pressure on neighboring China. As soon as the conflict with China was settled, Japan would withdraw all of its armed forces. Hull gave Namura to understand that despite Japan's stubbornness, the USA was considering delivering oil to Japan for civilian purposes, but he would like to see clear indications of Japan's peaceful intentions first.

The diplomats in the Japanese embassy were running out of time, because the Japanese government wanted agreement to be achieved with the USA by November 25. On November 22, however, Tōgō informed Nomura: "There are reasons beyond your ability to guess why we wanted to settle Japanese-American relations by the 25th. . . . If the signing can be completed by the 29th . . . we have decided to wait until that date." After that date, as the sinister-sounding message from the *Gaimushō* put it, "things are automatically going to happen."[113]

Nomura, who was relieved to learn of the extension of the deadline by a few days, was as unaware as Kurusu of the critical state of the military preparations in the Pacific. Japan had deployed warships, which had gathered on November 22 in Tankan Bay (*Hitokappuwan* in Japanese) in the Kuril Island of Iturup (*Etorofutō*) in the north-east of Japan. On November 26, this "mobile force" (*Kidō Butai*), consisting of six aircraft carriers with over 360 aircraft on board, along with two battleships, three cruisers, and nine destroyers as escorts, was to set sail for Pearl Harbor – hence November 25 as the deadline envisaged by Japan and communicated by Tōgō to the Japanese diplomats in Washington for an agreement. The fleet set off initially northward, where there were few ships in winter on account of the rough seas. The destroyers had been ordered to sink enemy ships immediately. Under no circumstances was the *Kidō Butai* to be discovered in advance. For that reason, complete radio silence was agreed. In order to make the American listening posts believe that Japan's warships, particularly the aircraft carriers, were still in Japanese waters, false radio signals were also transmitted from the Japanese coast. Both American and British intelligence were deceived in this way. The Allied secret services reported that the aircraft carriers *Akagi* and *Kaga* were in the south of Kyushu, the other four aircraft carriers in the *Kidō Butai* and the battleship *Kirishima* were near Kure, and the battleship *Hiei* was in Sasebo. The US government had as little idea as the Japanese diplomats in the Washington embassy of the threat that was approaching Pearl Harbor.[114]

The Hull Note

The negotiation showdown came finally on November 26 when Hull, visibly tired and debilitated by a stubborn head cold, handed Nomura and Kurusu the US government's official response to Japan's Plan B.[115] He had discussed a first draft in advance with the ambassadors of China and Great Britain and representatives of the Dutch government in exile. It demanded that Japan withdraw its troops from the south of French Indochina to restore the status before July 23, 1941, and that it guarantee that there would be a maximum of 25,000 Japanese soldiers in the north of French Indochina. In return, the USA offered to unfreeze Japanese assets and to restore economic relations with Japan.[116] A *modus vivendi* of this nature, which Roosevelt had already proposed to Nomura on November 10, would give the Americans more time to strengthen their defense in the Pacific – in the Philippines – and to continue to prepare for the war in Europe, which was becoming more and more likely.[117]

Hull's original plan had caused particular concern to the Chinese, who feared not only losing the support of the USA but also a weakening of the ABCD (American, British, Chinese, and Dutch) alliance against Japan.[118] Chiang Kai-shek sent a personal message to Roosevelt in that regard, protesting against the "disastrous" first draft. In contrast to the tirelessly propagated support for China over the previous four and a half years, the proposal was tantamount to a "betrayal" and would result in the collapse of China's resistance to Japan. In reaction to this protest note, Roosevelt, supported by his entire cabinet, had a new draft produced by Hull, who had been seeking a temporary compromise in order to gain time.[119]

The American position presented to Nomura and Kurusu on November 26 and known as the "Hull Note" was much harsher. Once again it contained the four Basic Principles that had been communicated to Japan at the start of the exploratory talks in April 1941 and had formed a leitmotif in the American demands.

Five further principles were formulated with a view to creating an economic basis for peace. The Hull Note also provided for the conclusion of a multilateral non-aggression pact by both countries with China, Great Britain, the Netherlands, the Soviet Union, and Thailand. Japan was to accept the territorial integrity of French Indochina and withdraw all of its military units from French Indochina and China. Both the USA and Japan should recognize Chiang Kai-shek's government and give up all extraterritorial rights in China. This was the American concession.[120]

The Hull Note represented the expression of the maximum demands made by the Americans and was diametrically opposed to the Japanese aims formulated in Plan B – as other participants were not slow to spot. During the preliminary talks, Ashley Clarke, a member of the British embassy in Tokyo, had warned the Foreign Office: "I think that we must also recognise that for the Japanese Government to have to inform their public at one blow that they had agreed to get out of Indo-China and China and dissociate themselves from the Axis and give up their co-prosperity ideas would be too much for any Japanese Government."[121] The contents of the Hull Note did indeed appear to the Japanese negotiators in Washington to be not a compromise but a veritable affront. For the Japanese government the terms were quite unacceptable.

From the American perspective, the Hull Note was fully in line with previous thrusts of US foreign policy. In 1928 the USA had co-signed the Kellogg-Briand Pact, which declared aggressive wars to be in violation of international law, thus clearly rejecting warfare as a foreign policy tool. In response to Japan's intervention in Manchuria and its occupation of north-east China, the USA had made clear in the Stimson Doctrine in 1932 that it would not recognize territorial expansion achieved by military force. Nomura thus interpreted the

Hull Note as a revised version of the Stimson Doctrine and hence as a general refusal to recognize Japan's territorial gains on the Chinese mainland. It could also be seen as a repeat of the Nine-Power Treaty of 1922, an international agreement that guaranteed China's territorial integrity and full national sovereignty.[122] Nomura also realized that Japan would not recall the Chinese government under Wang Jingwei that it had set up in Nanking.

Japan's representatives in Washington therefore rejected any formulation recognizing Chiang Kai-shek's government and a multilateral non-aggression pact – and hence the entire American proposal. Kurusu emphasized that Japan could not agree to this proposal and "take off its hat to Chiang Kai-shek"[123] by withdrawing its troops from China. Although the Hull Note never had a chance of being accepted, it was not officially rejected by Japan until December 7.

If Japan had accepted it, its gains in China would have been lost. The Note also seemed to demand Japan's permanent submission to the USA and Great Britain. Once the contents of the Hull Note were made known in Tokyo, even those who believed that Japan had little chance of winning a war against the USA became more fatalistic. The "hawk" faction saw the sharply worded Note as a welcome opportunity to persuade the Japanese people of the need for a war against the USA and to open hostilities. The advocates of peace found themselves with neither the arguments nor the energy to oppose the warmongers in their own country, since the American proposal offered no way out of the impasse into which diplomacy had maneuvered itself for months.

It should not be forgotten, however, that the Hull Note was a reaction to the inflexible attitude of the government in Tokyo, which had made no effort to find a consensus and seek a rapprochement with the American position. On the contrary, the Japanese government demanded that the USA lift all restrictions, while itself not agreeing to an immediate troop withdrawal but rather insisting on its own troops remaining in French Indochina and effectively reaffirming its territorial gains in China, the result of its expansionist policy. The Japanese were unaware that Hull personally regarded Japan's alliance with the German Reich as a genuine threat. Neither Konoe's nor Tōjō's government showed the slightest willingness to repudiate the Tripartite Pact, even partially, despite the opportunity to do so offered by the German invasion of the Soviet Union. Japan preferred to keep the option of war with the USA open, in the event that the Americans declared war on the Axis powers. The Japanese misjudged the US concerns, which tended to overestimate the potential of the Rome-Berlin-Tokyo alliance while underestimating Japan's military potential. Through its continued adhesion to the Tripartite Pact and the maintenance of a military presence in China and French Indochina, Japan was maintaining a scenario that threatened peace in the Pacific.

In this situation, the last hope for preservation of peace lay with the US president himself, whom Kurusu and Nomura asked to speak to immediately on receipt of the Hull Note. Roosevelt had shown himself to want peace and to be willing to meet Konoe, although the meeting never came about in the end. On November 25 Roosevelt had given Churchill advance warning of the official US reaction to Plan B. He considered the Hull Note to be a "fair offer," which Japan's politicians must now decide to accept or not. Roosevelt was pessimistic about its prospects, however. "I am not very hopeful and we must all be prepared for real trouble, possibly soon."[124] In his reply, Churchill gave his friend a free hand: "Of course, it is for you to handle this business and we certainly do not want an additional war."[125] He was also concerned about the possible "collapse of China," in other words its military defeat and capitulation to Japan, which would endanger the Anglo-American position in Asia. From Churchill's point of view, it was important to take account of China's interests and represent them in the negotiations. Apart from this, he had unconditional faith in Roosevelt.[126]

When Japan's representatives met the president on November 27, Roosevelt remained confrontational. Public opinion would not allow the economic restrictions on Japan to be eased as long as Japan did not make its peaceful intentions unmistakably clear. The president, too, seemed to have run out of patience. He was only too well aware of the consequences of rigid adherence to an appeasement course. In Europe it had merely allowed the German Reich to claim further territories and then to occupy them militarily. In winter 1941, Europe was in a situation of total war. It was necessary to prevent a similar situation developing in the Pacific, and for that reason the USA was now pursuing a harder line with Japan.[127]

On receipt of the Hull Note, the Japanese government considered Nomura and Kurusu's mission to have failed. In a communication to its diplomatic representations throughout the world, the *Gaimushō* stated on November 28 that peace negotiations with the USA were now over. Even after the deadline had expired, however, foreign minister Tōgō instructed Nomura and Kurusu on the same day to keep the lines to their American interlocutors open. They should not give the impression that the talks had finished but should emphasize that the Japanese government had offered the maximum concessions to the Americans, while the USA had shown no willingness to compromise and had hence rendered further negotiations impossible.

On November 29, the Emperor once again invited his

most important ministers and the traditional council of former prime ministers (*jūshin*), eight in all, to dinner. Three days earlier, Hirohito had warned against a possible war with the USA.[128] Before the final decision to go to war, he wanted to hear the *jūshin*'s opinion of the Hull Note. Unsurprisingly, Konoe was in favor of continuing to seek a peaceful solution – much more emphatically, in fact, than he had been while in office. The diverse opinions of the other participants made it appear so unlikely that the council would vote unequivocally in favor of a peaceful solution that the meeting was ultimately of little help to the Emperor in forming an opinion. Thus the last opportunity to exert influence on Hirohito as the final decision-making instance on whether to go to war or not remained unexploited.[129]

A last spark of hope for peace ignited for the Japanese diplomats in Washington on November 30. Through the mediation of Nishiyama Tsutomu, a tax official in New York, the Japanese embassy was in contact with a lawyer – referred to nebulously in Kurusu's memoirs as "Mr. D." – "a person with influence in political and financial circles in the USA."[130] He was the New York businessman Raoul E. Desvernine, who was indeed highly influential and known in the USA for his pro-Japanese attitude. As chairman of the Crucible Steel Company, he was keen to export steel to Manchukuo.[131] The Japanese envoy hoped that in the next few days Desvernine would be able to present the Japanese government's point of view to Roosevelt and convince him that a war with Japan, which would have far-reaching consequences and would trigger a world war, should be avoided at all costs.[132] Japan's diplomats in Washington failed to realize that Desvernine was not the best spokesperson to influence the president in their interests so late in the day. He was a well-connected and influential businessman but belonged to the right wing of the Republican camp. In a book published in the mid-1930s entitled *Democratic Despotism*,[133] he had fundamentally criticized Roosevelt's economic policy. At the beginning of December, therefore, Kurusu and Nomura were under the illusion that the president could be persuaded by one of his sharpest critics to rethink his position on Japan.

On November 30, Prince Takamatsu, recently transferred to navy operations, warned his brother Emperor Hirohito – who had himself expressed doubts a few days earlier about the wisdom of going to war – against a conflict with the USA. Members of the *Nihon Kaigun* were pessimistic about the possible outcome, and for that reason the navy still hoped to avoid war. The Emperor was unsettled and once again consulted with the two senior members of the navy, navy minister Shimada and chief-of-staff Nagano. Both assured him that the navy was ready for action and that they were not the slightest bit pessimistic.[134] At the fourth imperial conference of the year the following day, December 1, Emperor Hirohito approved the unanimous decision to go to war. For the Emperor, who in April 1941 had advised patience in the simmering conflict,[135] this was one more opportunity to steer a course away from confrontation and to prevent the outbreak of war in the Pacific. In the meantime, however, Hirohito had come round to the opinion of most of the political and military leaders. Very few believed in a Japanese victory over the USA, whose military and, above all, economic superiority was all too apparent. But in view of the listless diplomacy, a conviction had grown that a military collision between Japan and the USA would be inevitable sooner or later. The time now seemed ripe for this confrontation. The generally held view in Japan was "better now than later." Recalling the triumphant victory in the Russo-Japanese War of 1904/5, the majority of political and military leaders believed that a massive military strike at the start of the war followed by a tough and wearying war of attrition would persuade the USA to seek peace, with the idea of negotiating a settlement under better terms than had been possible in the diplomatic talks in 1941. In the absence of clear warnings by either the navy representatives or the *jūshin*, the Emperor agreed to the war that had already been voted for by the high command and government. Even though it was customary for the Emperor merely to rubber-stamp decisions that had already been adopted, he still had the opportunity here to intervene in the process. By relying on the judgment of his political and military leadership, Emperor Hirohito refused to take personal responsibility and, in spite of his private desire for peace, did not plead for a negotiated solution with the USA. The imperial conference as an institution had ensured that the few supporters of peace who had waited for the Emperor to pronounce in their favor had not raised their voices clearly. As no one was strongly and emphatically opposed to the war, the leaders in Japan had literally "slid" into a war situation.

In the late morning of December 1, 1941, Fala, the US president's faithful black Scottish Terrier, trotted through the corridors of the White House – a clear indication that the president was in residence. Roosevelt had left on November 27 to spend a few days in his country retreat, the Little White House in Warm Springs, Georgia, but had returned to Washington earlier than expected. The president's press office did not explain why Roosevelt had cut short his vacation.[136] Perhaps he had been concerned about the speech given on November 29 by the Japanese prime minister Tōjō, which had been reported the following day by the US media. In this speech, Tōjō had complained about the interference of various nations, including the USA and Great Britain, which was preventing the establishment of a "welfare sphere" in east Asia. His tone had been aggressive, demanding the expulsion of the British

and Americans from Asia "in an act of retaliation."[137]
He appeared to be committed to aggression – for the
moment in words only. In October he had already
stated in a private conversation with Konoe: "Once
in a lifetime, one must show courage, close one's eyes
and jump from the terrace of the Kiyomizu-dera."[138]
He was referring to the Japanese proverb stating that
the wishes of a person who survived the jump from the
terrace of the Buddhist temple in Kyoto would come
true.[139] Implicitly he was comparing the decision to go
to war with a leap into the unknown, while expressing
his hope that the wishes of the nation would come true.
Although the outcome of the impending war was uncertain, Japan was now determined to accept the risk of a
military defeat rather than abandon without a struggle
the territory acquired in China as a result of its aggressive expansion policy.

   In early December the American people were still
largely unaware of the imminent threat of war in Asia.
The media had long focused more on the western hemisphere and the German Reich as a potential opponent in
war. Public opinion was split on the question of whether
to enter the war in Europe. The opponents wished to
keep the USA out of a war with the German Reich.[140]
According to *Life* magazine, very few American citizens
seriously believed in early December 1941 in a war
between Japan and the USA. If the Japanese Empire
were to take up arms in the Pacific, its activities would
be directed in the first instance against the British pos-
sessions in Asia – Singapore, Hong Kong, or Rangoon.
America's journalists indulged in wild speculation. The
evening edition of the liberal daily *The Boston Globe*,
for example, reported on the training of Japanese par-
achutists in Kwangtung, China, and conjectured an
imminent Japanese invasion from French Indochina of
neighboring Thailand or the Dutch East Indies.[141] At this
time the American press knew nothing of the Hull Note.

On December 2, Under Secretary of State Welles handed Nomura and Kurusu a letter from Roosevelt, who had been informed by US intelligence of the massing of a large number of Japanese troops in French Indochina. Roosevelt asked the Japanese government to reveal its intentions. Nomura informed Welles that Japan was forced to protect its own interests on account of the economic pressure exerted by the USA.

Three days later, Nomura and Kurusu submitted the official reply from Tokyo, stating that Japan had to reinforce its armed forces in the north of French Indochina as a precautionary measure, as Chinese troops were active in the area bordering China. Hull objected that a possible attack by the Chinese on French Indochina would be a further reason for Japan to withdraw its units, in response to which the two Japanese diplomats demanded that the USA should cease its support of China as soon as a Sino-Japanese peace process was initiated. Hull asked whether in return Japan would also cease its support for Hitler. "This isn't getting us anywhere," [142] those present heard Nomura murmur in annoyance. All of his efforts over the previous months to achieve some kind of agreement between Washington and Tokyo had been in vain.

In order to attempt once again to break the stalemate, Roosevelt took the initiative on the evening of December 6 and sent a personal message to Emperor Hirohito expressing his final hopes for peace. He had already sent a message to the Emperor in mid-October, when the idea was being discussed of a meeting between Konoe and Roosevelt. Considering that Japan might turn against the Soviet Union, he had urgently warned the Japanese against starting a new war. Four years earlier, on December 13, 1937, when Japanese bombers sank the American gunboat USS Panay in Chinese waters, Roosevelt had been in direct contact with Hirohito. His conversation at the time had helped to resolve the crisis:

Japan officially apologized for the incident and paid compensation.[143]

In his letter of December 6, Roosevelt now emphasized the American hope that the conflict between China and Japan could be settled and peace restored to the Pacific. The aim of his government was the peaceful coexistence of all nations in the region and the implementation of the principle of economic equality. Roosevelt criticized the threatening troop movements in the south of French Indochina and demanded that Japan withdraw its troops from there so as to ensure peace. At the same time, he gave his assurance that neither American nor other – Chinese, for example – units had the intention of invading French Indochina themselves after the withdrawal of the Japanese troops. Although the tone of the letter was basically friendly and Roosevelt made explicit reference to the friendly relations between the two countries that had existed for almost a century, he made it quite clear to the Emperor that if Japan continued on its current course, war would inevitably follow.[144]

On December 6, Roosevelt also informed Viscount Halifax, the British ambassador in Washington, that he had sent a message to Emperor Hirohito. If no reply was received by the evening of December 8, Washington time, or if the reply was "unsatisfactory," the US government would issue a warning to the Japanese the following day. The US president also advised the British government and the Dutch government in exile in London to follow the US example on the following day so as to increase the pressure on Japan.[145] The USA was now also heading for war, and time was running out to avoid it. No doubt to prevent a peace initiative quite literally at the last moment, the Japanese general staff had ordered the telegraph office in Tokyo to delay delivery of the important personal message from the US president to the Emperor by almost half a day. The audience that US ambassador Grew had hoped for to present Roosevelt's telegram in person to the Emperor thus never took place.[146]

Japan's official reply to the Hull Note also arrived on December 6. The fourteen-point letter contained a summary of the course of the bilateral talks to date from the Japanese point of view. It emphasized that Japan had always sought peace, while the USA had adopted a problematic imperialist stance. It concluded that agreement with the USA would not be possible, even if the talks were to continue.[147] Effectively, Japan was notifying the end of diplomatic talks, even if it did not yet officially declare war.

Nomura and Kurusu, who were left in the dark by their own government until the last moment regarding the imminent outbreak of war, were instructed to hand over the letter to the US government at precisely 1 p.m. Washington time. At that time it would be 7.30 a.m. in Hawaii, a few minutes after sunrise – and shortly before the start of the Japanese aerial attack on Pearl Harbor.[148] The Japanese embassy was also ordered to destroy the encrypting machine, all codebooks, and all confidential documents after deciphering the message, which, like all telegrams between the *Gaimushō* and the embassy, had been sent in a special diplomatic code.

Fatefully, the embassy staff did not decipher the message competently. As the last part of the encrypted message was sent from Tokyo much later, a readable version of the telegram was not available until well after 1 p.m. With this deciphered version of the Japanese reply, ambassador Nomura and special envoy Kurusu made their way to the State Department, arriving just after 2 p.m. After a short time, they were met by a sombre-faced Hull. He had just received a telephone call from Roosevelt, who had briefly relayed to him: "There's a report that the Japanese have attacked Pearl Harbor."[149] This phone call had seriously unsettled Hull, and he only received the two Japanese at 2.20 p.m.

because the report of the attack had not yet been confirmed. He already knew the contents of the reply from
Tokyo. As Nomura had long suspected, US intelligence
had been intercepting Japan's diplomatic communications for several months. This time the Americans had
deciphered the government's official reply more rapidly
than the embassy staff. After cursorily glancing at the
message for the sake of form, he said angrily to Kurusu
and Nomura: "In all my fifty years of public service I
have never seen a document that was more crowded
with infamous falsehoods and distortions – infamous
falsehoods and distortions on a scale so huge that I
never imagined until today that any Government on
this planet was capable of uttering them."[150] With these
words, he threw the surprised Japanese diplomats out of
his office. Hull's fear was soon confirmed: the Japanese
naval air force had attacked Pearl Harbor.

2

The Japanese War Plan

Admiral Yamamoto and Operation Hawaii

After the Japanese government decided on November 5, 1941, to attack the US naval base in Pearl Harbor should the authorities in Washington and Tokyo fail to reach a diplomatic agreement, several warships put to sea on November 26 from the Kuril Islands in the north of Japan.[1] This fleet, known as the *Kidō Butai* ("mobile force") was commanded by Vice Admiral Nagumo Chūichi. Assembled through the creation of the 1st Air Fleet of the imperial Japanese navy on April 10, 1941, it consisted originally of five aircraft carriers.[2] A further aircraft carrier was added in winter 1941. The flagship was the *Akagi* ("Red Castle"), albeit more for traditional reasons than on account of its greater performance. Named for a Japanese volcano, its outdated anti-aircraft batteries, the small number of aircraft hangars, and the lower sea endurance in fact made it a weaker carrier in the fleet in terms of military combat strength. It was launched in 1925 and carried sixty-three aircraft, including eighteen Mitsubishi A6M2 fighter aircraft, described as "Model 0" (*reisen*) and destined to become renowned under the name "Zero." For the most part, however, the *Akagi* carried bomber aircraft. After they had delivered their destructive payload, the eighteen highly maneuverable Aichi D3A dive bombers were expected to support the Zero fighters in a possible aerial battle with US fighter aircraft over Hawaii. The twenty-seven Nakajima B5N torpedo bombers, the largest group on board the *Akagi*, were to be part of the first assault wave, escorted by nine Zero fighters. Together with the aircraft carrier *Kaga*, named for a Japanese province and with a capacity of seventy aircraft, the *Akagi* and other escort ships formed the First Carrier Division.

A Mitsubishi A6M Zero fighter about to take off from the deck of a Japanese navy aircraft carrier during the Battle of the Santa Cruz Islands (October 25–27, 1942). The Zero fighter took part in almost every major action in which the Japanese navy was committed. It was an extremely maneuverable aircraft and had an exceptional range, which made it the symbol of Japanese air power. (Frame enlargement from AWM Film No. F06922, Frame 20024.)

The Second Carrier Division was made up of the smaller but more technically advanced Dragon aircraft carriers *Sōryū* ("Sapphire Blue Dragon") and *Hiryū* ("Flying Dragon"), whose relatively large aircraft capacity and armor plating made them much more effective in combat. The fifth and sixth carriers in the mobile force were Cranes – the *Shōkaku* ("Flying Crane") and its identical sister ship *Zuikaku* ("Happy Crane") – named for the Japanese symbol of luck and long life. These two new Shōkaku-class vessels had only been completed in August and September 1941, respectively. They could each carry up to eighty-four aircraft and together formed the Fifth Carrier Division of the *Kidō Butai*.[3] Apart from the three Carrier Divisions, each with two carriers and over 350 aircraft on board, the fleet also included two battleships, two heavy cruisers and one light cruiser, nine destroyers, and five submarines.

The *Kidō Butai* was put together in this way to carry out Operation Hawaii, a military operation that formed an essential component of the large-scale Japanese war plan in the Asia-Pacific region. Through its surprise attack on Pearl Harbor, the Japanese government sought to neutralize the US Pacific Fleet, which had been stationed there permanently since May 1940. Parallel to and immediately following the attack on Pearl Harbor, Japan's army and navy were to advance in December 1941 to occupy further territories in south-east Asia and a number of islands in the Pacific. The Japanese war plan aimed to secure areas of south-east Asia rich in raw materials and to advance in the west as far as the eastern border of India so as to put the British Empire under pressure. The annexation of Burma, Malaya, Borneo, and the bases in Hong Kong and Singapore would secure strategic military and geographical areas of the Japanese Empire in Asia. To the south, it would occupy New Guinea, posing a direct threat to Australia in this way as well. The Japanese also wanted to take Guam, the Philippines, and Wake Atoll, important US bases in the Pacific. The large-scale Japanese campaign of conquest in south-east Asia depended on the ability of the surprise air raid to extensively neutralize the US Pacific Fleet at anchor in Pearl Harbor. If it failed, it would be met by an immediate massive counterattack by the US navy.

The mastermind behind Operation Hawaii was Admiral Yamamoto Isoroku.[4] Born in 1884 in Nagaoka in Niigata prefecture into a poor former samurai family, he was named Takano Isoroku, for his father's age when he was born (isoroku = fifty-six). After joining the Japanese navy, he served as a young cadet on the armored cruiser *Nisshin* and was seriously wounded in the battle of Tsushima, losing two fingers on his left hand. Following his exceptional performance in the navy academy, he was adopted by the time-honored Nagaoka-based Yamamoto clan. From then on he took the name Yamamoto Isoroku. He studied in the USA as a young navy officer, discovering the country and traveling extensively from there to Mexico and Cuba. Thanks to his excellent English, he was attached to the Japanese delegation as an America expert at the London Naval Conference in 1930. In the light of his experience, Yamamoto was favorably inclined towards the USA and was against going to war with it.[5] Apart from this anglo-phile attitude, Yamamoto, who loved strategy games like go, poker, and bridge, had a very clear conception of military operations. It was this that led to his promotion to First Admiral and to his becoming a Japanese *strategos*. Unlike the three-service system – army, navy, and air force – in the German Reich, Japan's military was based on the army and navy, each with its own air force. Yamamoto quickly recognized the importance in modern warfare of air forces in general, and of naval air forces and aircraft carriers in maritime warfare in particular. After holding various positions in the naval air force – he had in the meantime become commander of the aircraft carrier *Akagi* – Yamamoto ascended the military career ladder to the highest rung. In 1937 he was appointed deputy minister of the navy and subsequently became the spokesman for the left-leaning faction in the navy. He was against the army's expansionist policy and rapprochement with Nazi Germany. Yamamoto correctly predicted that an alliance with Germany would inevitably lead to war with the USA in the Pacific, which Japan could not win on account of its inferior military and economic strength. As political assassinations were no rarity in the late 1930s in Japan, and Yamamoto as a politician – and possibly a future minister of the navy – was particularly vulnerable to an attack by ultra-nationalists, in 1939 the equally pro-American prime minister Yonai Mitsumasa appointed him commander-in-chief of the Combined Fleet. He was promoted to admiral on November 15, 1940, and had thus reached the peak of his career in December 1941, while the preparations for war with the USA were in progress. Moderate forces in naval circles, by whom he was highly appreciated, had cleverly and skillfully ensured that he stayed out of politics so as to protect him from attack. Yamamoto was now the most important military man in the Japanese navy.

Shortly before war broke out with the USA, Yamamoto wrote to a friend: "A decision [to go to war] has been made that is diametrically opposed to my attitude as an individual. There is no other choice but to pursue this course with determination and energy. This current situation is indeed strange for me. I suppose I should regard it as my destiny."[6]

It may indeed be seen as an irony of history that Yamamoto of all people, who was a member of the "dove" faction in the navy, should now, in his position as commander-in-chief of the Combined Fleet, have to seriously consider how to wage and win a war against the USA. It is not known when he first conceived the idea for the Hawaii operation and the scenario of a pre-emptive attack on the US Pacific Fleet. It is possible that he was inspired by trial maneuvers in March 1940, which simulated an attack by aircraft from the carrier *Sōryū* on the Nagato-class battleships *Mutsu* and *Nagato*. The eighty-one aircraft from the First Carrier Division commanded by Ozawa Jisaburō clearly demonstrated to Yamamoto the effectiveness of a coordinated aerial attack by fighters, and torpedo and dive bombers. He commented to Fukudome Shigeru, chief-of-staff of the Combined Fleet at the time, who was observing the exercise from the flagship *Nagato*: "Wouldn't it be possible to attack Hawaii from the air?"[7] The idea of an aerial attack on Pearl Harbor might well have been born in this context.[8]

The assumption by the commander-in-chief of the Combined Fleet that the air force was the decisive factor in modern maritime warfare was reinforced by the two-wave British Royal Navy air raid in the night of November 11–12, 1940, which inflicted a serious blow on the Italian navy stationed in Taranto, Italy. The Swordfish biplane torpedo bombers, which took off from the aircraft carrier *HMS Illustrious*, disabled half the battleships of the Italian fleet from the air. The vulnerability of large battleships to air attack was seen again in May 1941, when the Royal Navy sank the *Bismarck*, the flagship of the German navy.

Before and in parallel to these events, Yamamoto had young navy officers trained as fighter pilots in the navy air force. Within the *Nihon Kaigun*, Yamamoto was therefore on the side of the modern-thinking, younger navy officers who had become convinced by the Battle of Taranto that enemy ships in the Pacific could also be defeated primarily through air attacks. Recalling the glorious victory in the Battle of Tsushima in May

Admiral Yamamoto Isoroku, the commander-in-chief
of the Combined Fleet, planned Operation Hawaii,
although he himself warned strongly against a war
with the USA.

Tailandier/Bridgeman Images

1905, however, some of the older Japanese admirals
were still of the traditional view that the next sea battle
in the Pacific would also be conducted and won with a
large fleet of ships. After the elimination of the Russian

fleet in Tsushima, the Royal Navy and, even more so, the US navy, were seen as Japan's potential enemies at sea. To be able to compete with the latter, the supporters of a pure naval battle advocated the construction of even larger, more powerful, and faster battleships with greater firepower. The launch of the two Yamato-class superships, *Yamato* in August and *Musashi* in November 1940, reflected the belief that predominated in the *Nihon Kaigun* at the time.

Yamamoto himself was a supporter of the new military strategy. In a private letter to navy minister Oikawa Koshirō on January 7, 1941, regarding the preparations for a potential war, he put down in writing for the first time his idea of attacking the US Pacific Fleet in Hawaii from the air and also with submarines. The letter indicates that he had spoken to the minister previously about this scenario. "I would very much like to be appointed commander of an aircraft carrier fleet so as to be able to give the order myself for such an attack,"[9] he continued. Yamamoto's express wish to be demoted from commander-in-chief of the Combined Fleet to commander of an aircraft carrier fleet reveals the extent to which he was fascinated by the revolutionary idea of an aerial attack on an enemy fleet.[10]

In mid-January 1941, Yamamoto initiated some of the Combined Fleet staff into his strategy considerations. He explained his scenario of a pre-emptive strike compared with the traditional concept of a decisive battle: the American Pacific Fleet was to be rendered inoperative not at sea but in the Philippines or on Hawaii. Captain Kuroshima Kameto, a Combined Fleet staff officer and friend of Yamamoto, commissioned commander Sasaki Akira to study the possibilities for attacking Hawaii. Sasaki presented three scenarios.[11] The first had dive bombers taking off from aircraft carriers 350 sea miles (650 km) away. Assuming the Americans had defensive positions in place, the airplanes would attack only the US aircraft carriers, while leaving the battleships unscathed. The second scenario also had an attack exclusively with dive bombers, but in this case they were to land in the sea after the attack, with the crews to be picked up by submarines. This scenario was intended above all to protect the Japanese carrier fleet. Abandoning the aircraft would make it impossible to give away the location of the aircraft carriers, protecting them in this way from an American counterattack. The loss of the dive bombers in the sea had the considerable disadvantage that they could not be used for a second operation. As the crew rescue was extremely dependent on the weather and could not therefore be guaranteed, this plan was quickly discarded. According to the third scenario, Japanese aircraft carriers would advance to a distance of 300 sea miles (550 km), from where a combined attack with fighter aircraft, dive bombers, and torpedo bombers could be launched. This scenario had strong similarities to another plan that Yamamoto had commissioned in parallel, so as to take as much advantage as possible of the diverse opinions of air force experts. At the end of January 1941, he had commissioned Rear Admiral Ōnishi Takijirō to submit his ideas for an attack on Hawaii. Recently appointed chief-of-staff of the 11th Air Fleet of the Japanese navy, Ōnishi had commanded several air battles on the Chinese front and hence had considerable experience of aerial warfare.

In early February Ōnishi contacted commander Genda Minoru, who was on board the aircraft carrier *Kaga* anchored in Shibushi Bay in the south of the Japanese island of Kyushu. Genda was an ace fighter pilot and a staff officer on the carrier, which was part of the First Carrier Division. Admiral Yamamoto had written to him: "If we go to war with the USA and fail to destroy the US fleet in Hawaii, there is no chance that we will win. And even if we do destroy it, there is still no certainty that we will win. This operation [against the US Pacific Fleet] is in any case essential. The attack is to be carried out by the First and Second Carrier Divisions. Please investigate how feasible this is."[12] A week later, Genda presented two plans for the attack. Both had the US base being attacked in two waves. The aircraft were to fly back and forth between the aircraft carriers and Hawaii so as to strike repeatedly. To achieve the highest possible hit rate, Genda's first plan was confined to dive bombers, since at the time horizontal and torpedo bombardment – for example with Nakajima B5N aircraft – was not yet fully developed in Japan. Because they were dropped from a great height, the torpedoes sank deep into the water. For a harbor as shallow as Pearl Harbor – just 12 meters – torpedo bombers were useless. If the technical problems could be solved, Genda's second plan provided for a combined attack by dive bombers and torpedo bombers – as in Sasaki's scenario.

In both of Genda's plans, fighter aircraft were to escort the bombers to protect them from enemy fighters and then to attack the aircraft facilities on the American base. In both scenarios, enemy aircraft carriers were seen as the primary target. Battleships, cruisers, auxiliary vessels, and the aircraft facilities and other infrastructure on land were also to be attacked, but only as secondary targets. Genda's proposal to attack all of Pearl Harbor was rejected from the outset.[13] The US navy aircraft carriers were targeted in particular to prevent an immediate counterattack and hence to ensure the safety of the Japanese carrier fleet. Genda's plan called for three carrier divisions, the aircraft carriers *Akagi* and *Kaga* as the First Carrier Division, *Hiryū* and *Sōryū* as the Second, and *Ryūjō* as the Fourth Division.[14] In this way Genda was looking to employ all of the aircraft carriers in the *Nihon Kaigun* available at the time. As potential rendezvous points he suggested first Hokkaido, the most northerly of the main Japanese islands, alternatively the Ogasawara islands a good 1,000 km south of Tokyo. Within two weeks the fleet would be 200 sea miles (370 km) from Hawaii, from where the attack was to be launched.

Genda's plan for a combined attack with torpedo and dive bombers was rejected by Ōnishi, who said that in view of the relatively shallow water in Pearl Harbor, torpedo bombers were out of the question. He also presumed that there would be a torpedo net to protect the ships at anchor. He suggested a scenario to Yamamoto using only dive bombers, but this was also rejected. Yamamoto believed that an attack with just dive bombers would not be highly effective. He stubbornly insisted on Genda's idea of a combined attack. Yamamoto's support of this plan considerably increased its chance of being accepted. The details now had to be worked out, fine-tuned for months at the Combined Fleet headquarters. The "Operation Plan for a Surprise Attack on Hawaii" was to be elaborated in particular by Ōnishi, chief-of-staff of the 11th Air Fleet, Kusaka Ryūnosuke, chief-of-staff of the 1st Air Fleet, and Genda. They were also to plan the supply ship deployment and the precise route. As the two Crane-class aircraft carriers were close to completion, they were also included in the plan.[15]

While Yamamoto was working on the plan for attacking Hawaii, in August 1941 the prospect of war with the USA has risen considerably after the US government had imposed an embargo on Japan a month earlier following the invasion by Japanese troops of the south of French Indochina. The general staff of the imperial navy under Admiral Nagano Ōsami was refining its plans in the summer of 1941 for a coordinated attack in the Asia-Pacific region against the USA and Great Britain, and had also received a first proposal for Operation Hawaii from Yamamoto's headquarters. In discussions with Kuroshima Kameto, the senior

Combined Fleet staff officer, however, the navy general staff advised against Yamamoto's proposal. With the two-week voyage to Hawaii, it was highly likely that the Japanese fleet would be discovered by enemy ships and airplanes; in addition, the fuel supply for the carrier fleet was not certain. And finally, an aerial attack on Pearl Harbor involved considerable technical difficulties. Using horizontal bombers, which would release their deadly payload from an altitude of around 2,000 meters, the accuracy was likely to be low, and if there was heavy cloud or bad weather, an air raid with bombs would not be possible. In view of the size of the American battleships, the destruction potential of the dive bombers was relatively small. Above all, however, the aircraft carriers would be needed for the Japanese advance in south-east Asia and could not therefore be used against Hawaii. The navy general staff concluded that the plan proposed by the Combined Fleet was too speculative and had too little promise of success. For the time being, in summer 1941, the *Nihon Kaigun* repeatedly rejected the idea of attacking Pearl Harbor.

Yamamoto nevertheless stuck to his plan and continued to refine his idea of an aerial attack. In September 1941, the Combined Fleet headquarters simulated the scenario of a war with the USA in the Pacific in the naval war college in Meguro, Tokyo. The plan for attacking Hawaii was also revised once again in detail. Yamamoto and his staff presented the results to the representatives of the navy general staff. The *Kidō Butai* would approach the main Hawaiian island of Oahu and Pearl Harbor from the north. The core of the fleet would consist of the four aircraft carriers from the First and Second Carrier Divisions, escorted by two heavy cruisers, eight destroyers, and nineteen submarines. A total of 360 aircraft would be in operation. The military scenario played out on a map envisaged the sinking of four US battleships, two aircraft carriers, and three cruisers, and the infliction of heavy damage on one battleship, an aircraft carrier, and three cruisers. By the end of the operation, 180 American aircraft would be destroyed. Although the Japanese would also suffer considerable losses – it was estimated that one aircraft carrier would be seriously damaged and 217 aircraft lost – overall Operation Hawaii would be successful, as the drawing-board simulation showed.[16]

As Yamamoto was now asking for the use of six aircraft carriers following the completion of the new Crane-class vessels, but the navy general staff was still generally opposed to Operation Hawaii, Ōnishi and Kusaka, chiefs-of-staff of the 11th and 1st Air Fleets, offered a compromise solution. Because the sea was generally rough and the weather bad in the north, supplying fuel to the ships would be a problem. It was therefore suggested that perhaps only the two new Crane-class carriers, *Shōkaku* and *Zuikaku*, along with the *Kaga*, should be used for the attack on Hawaii. These three aircraft carriers had a range of 10,000 sea miles and could thus reach their destination without additional fuel. As the pilots from the two Shōkaku-class aircraft carriers were inexperienced and still in training, they should be replaced by experienced pilots from the *Sōryū* and *Hiryū*. These two carriers, along with the *Akagi*, should not take part in the attack on Hawaii but should be used for the campaign in south-east Asia. This distribution represented a compromise between the navy general staff and Yamamoto's demand for all six aircraft carriers to be used against Pearl Harbor. Under these circumstances, however, the force of the attack would be limited, with only 226 aircraft, over 100 fewer than proposed by Admiral Yamamoto. In his opinion, this was not enough to ensure the success of the attack on the US Pacific Fleet, for which he demanded at least 350 bombers and fighter aircraft. Arguing against Ōnishi and Kusaka's compromise, he said: "What will we do

if during the military operation in south-east Asia an
aerial attack by the US fleet comes from the east? If our
access to natural resources in south-east Asia is blocked
and the Americans get their hands on them – there
will also be scorched earth in Tokyo and Osaka. I am
only the commander of the Combined Fleet, but I urge
most strongly that the surprise attack on Hawaii take
place."[17] Yamamoto continued to insist on six aircraft
carriers being used against Hawaii, even after further
studies in October 1941 suggested that the *Nihon
Kaigun* would lose half of the materiel employed in the
attack on Pearl Harbor. But the proud commander-in-
chief of the Combined Fleet was unwilling to present
a compromise solution to the navy general staff. He
would not budge an inch, maintaining that if an attack
on Hawaii were to take place – which as a pro-American
he was not in favor of in the first place – it should be in
accordance with his plans.

Just a few hours after Tōjō's new cabinet convened
on October 19, Yamamoto's staff officer Kuroshima
Kameto once again met Fukudome Shigeru, head of
the first department of the navy general staff, which
was responsible for military operations and war strategy. Kameto insisted that in the event of a war with
the USA, Operation Hawaii using six aircraft carriers should be reconsidered. Rear Admiral Fukudome
adamantly opposed the idea, saying that if Operation
Hawaii were to take place at all, then it should involve
just four aircraft carriers. Kuroshima then demanded
to speak with Rear Admiral Itō Seiichi, who had
only been deputy navy chief-of-staff since September.
Kuroshima was a good friend of Itō, who like
Yamamoto was an anglophile and until a few weeks
earlier had been the chief-of-staff of the Combined
Fleet. Kuroshima presented Yamamoto's demand that
Operation Hawaii take place with six aircraft carriers, playing his last trump card by threatening: "If

you refuse to accept the Operation Hawaii plan, Yamamoto will resign as commander of the Combined Fleet." Itō was visibly perturbed by this threat and asked Kuroshima to wait. He fetched Nagano Ōsami, who opined: "If Yamamoto is so keen to implement Operation Hawaii that he would abandon his command of the Combined Fleet, the operation should take place according to his wishes. But he will bear full responsibility for it." Admiral Yamamoto thus won out against the navy general staff, which the next day decided to step up preparations for war. At the same time, the Imperial Navy Operation Plan was approved, including Operation Hawaii.[18]

At the liaison conference on November 15, 1941, Japan's military and political decision-makers decided on the country's war plan, which had been agreed ten days earlier at the imperial conference in the event that diplomatic negotiations with Washington should fail. The plan envisaged the conquest of large parts of the Pacific Asian region within five months. The second phase would call for the defense of the occupied territories, from Burma to the Bismarck Archipelago, securing natural resources, and finally, through a war of attrition, forcing the USA to negotiate for peace. Yamamoto's Operation Hawaii, which was presented to the Emperor by Admiral Nagano on November 4, played a central role in this war plan. Parallel to the advance on the Malayan peninsula and the Philippines, the second major US base in the Pacific, an attack was to be carried out on the US Pacific Fleet anchored in Pearl Harbor, marking the start of the war in the Pacific.[19]

The plan of attack

After the general staff had agreed to Operation Hawaii, the 1st Air Fleet set about making a detailed plan

Vice Admiral Nagumo Chūichi, Japanese 1st Air Fleet.
Courtesy National Archives, photo no. 12009118

of attack.[20] For the *Kidō Butai* commanded by Vice Admiral Nagumo, consisting of six aircraft carriers, as Yamamoto had demanded, the weather was stable and favorable for an approach to Hawaii from the Marshall Islands. However, there was a great danger of being discovered by American patrol boats or merchant ships. Ultimately, a route through the north Pacific was chosen. The sea there was much rougher and the weather worse, but the area north of 40° latitude was no longer patrolled by the US navy and was well away from the usual shipping routes. The weather and shipping there and around the island of Hawaii was studied in detail and a route decided. The ships of the *Kidō Butai* would gather in Tankan Bay (*Hitokappuwan*) in Iturup (*Etorofutō*) in the Kuril Islands, sail north and move east on the line of 42° latitude to 800 sea miles (1,500 km) east of the Midway Islands. Four days before the attack, they would be put on full alert for enemy aircraft, as the danger of being discovered by American patrols and being attacked from the air increased as the fleet neared Hawaii. The ships were now to veer south-east, arriving at the intersection of 33°N and 157°W on the day before the attack. In the early morning of the day of the attack the Japanese aircraft carriers were to approach a position 200 sea miles (370 km) north of Pearl Harbor while – as Japanese spies had reported – an air patrol from the US fleet set off south from Oahu.[21]

From this point, the first of two waves of the combined aerial attack – consisting according to Yamamoto's plan of 350 fighters, horizontal and dive bombers – was to leave an hour before sunrise. Escorted by Zero fighters, the bombers were to fly in squadrons to their target, the main Hawaiian island of Oahu, which the Japanese war planners had divided into five attack zones. The first zone consisted of the area between the naval yard and Ford Island; the second was the area north-west of Ford Island; East Loch, Middle Loch, and West Loch were the three other zones. The first zone was further subdivided into the docks north-west of the naval yard, where the US Pacific Fleet battleships were anchored, the harbor area, where other ships were anchored or being repaired, the harbor facilities, and the remaining area. This first zone, in which the attackers had located most of the Pacific Fleet, the battleships, and aircraft carriers, was the main point of attack. As the pilots of the First and Second Carrier Division squadrons were highly trained and experienced, they were to attack the US battleships in the core area, while the much less experienced pilots of the Fifth Carrier Division were to attack the airfields and ground facilities.

Because there was not enough room on the aircraft carriers to enable all of the planes to take off at the same time, a maneuver that would in any case have required too much time and coordination to form up as a squadron in the air, Japan's war plan, at Genda's insistence in particular, provided for a second wave to set off ninety minutes after the first wave from the *Kidō Butai*, which would already be moving slowly northward at this time. After the two waves had been launched, the fleet was to proceed at a speed of 20 knots (37 km/h) for its own protection to a point 300 sea miles (550 km) north of Pearl Harbor so as to be out of range of American aircraft taking off from Hawaii. This calculation had been based on the maximum range of 1,100 km of the US Consolidated PBY Catalina reconnaissance aircraft. Genda had adamantly opposed this plan, since by steadily moving away to the north, the aircraft carriers would soon be too far away for damaged Japanese aircraft to return to them. A plan based on withdrawal and protection only for the aircraft carriers would also have a negative effect on crew morale. Genda's objections were ultimately taken into account by having the *Kidō Butai* fleet continue southward after the launch of the first attack wave 230 sea miles (426 km) north of Pearl Harbor so that the second wave could be launched from a distance of 200 sea miles (370 km) and only then turning north. Although the undertaking was riskier for the carrier fleet, the planes would have a much easier route back to aircraft carriers.

After the aircraft had returned, the *Kidō Butai* was to pass Midway, 800 sea miles (1,500 km) away and return to the Japanese inland sea. Should the fleet have been slightly damaged by a counterattack, the Second

Fuchida Mitsuo, who had been made frigate captain
a few weeks previously, commanded the first wave of
Japan's attack on Pearl Harbor on December 7, 1941.

Keystone-France/Getty

(*Hiryū*, *Sōryū*) and Fifth (*Shōkaku*, *Zuikaku*) Carrier
Divisions should each be reduced by one aircraft carrier.
The planes on these two aircraft carriers would then
attack the US naval base on Midway, ensure control of
the airspace, and enable the fleet to return in this way
by the shortest route. If the fleet were to suffer heavy
damage, it would have to retreat to the mandate territory of the Marshall Islands.

Although refueling the aircraft carriers at sea in the
north Pacific was particularly difficult on account of
the wintry weather in November and December, seven
10,000-ton tankers accompanied the fleet. The refueling of the aircraft carriers was practiced intensively
during maneuvers, as it was essential that the ships of
the "mobile force" had sufficient fuel. They could not
call into port, because the premature discovery of the

Kidō Butai had to be avoided at all costs. In case the fleet could not be refueled on the high seas, 3,500 metal drums each containing 200 liters of heavy oil to drive the large diesel engines and 40,000 oil cans each with 18 liters of light oil were carried on the aircraft carriers.[22]

It was originally discussed whether the planes should take off in the night so as to surprise the US Pacific Fleet while it was sleeping. In maneuvers, however, it was discovered that while take off in the dark was no problem, it proved difficult to form the aircraft into squadrons when in the air. The organization of a coordinated attack involving the Nakajima B5N horizontal and torpedo bombers with their armor-piercing torpedoes and the Aichi D3A dive bombers with 250 kg bombs was also much more difficult at night. The experienced pilots in the First and Second Carrier Divisions could be relied on to fly in formation, but not the less experienced pilots of the Fifth Carrier Division. For that reason, the flight plan was adapted and the first wave was scheduled to take off an hour before sunrise.

Fuchida Mitsuo, born in 1902 in the Year of the Tiger, a symbol of good leadership, and commander of the flying squadron on the *Akagi* and the aircraft in the First Carrier Division, was chosen to command and coordinate the first attack wave.[23] He had attended the navy academy in Etajima at the same time as Prince Takamatsu, and met another cadet there, Gendu Minoru, who was from a samurai family. Fuchida had deliberately chosen English rather than French or German as a foreign language so as to learn more about the US navy, the Japanese navy's potential main enemy. Because he blushed easily, as a child he was nicknamed "Tako," octopus. But then a man entered the political stage in Europe, Adolf Hitler, whose career he followed with great admiration. Fuchida, whose moustache was similar to Hitler's, soon earned the new nickname "Hitler." He won his military spurs during the Sino-

Japanese War in the late 1930s and became one of
the best and most experienced fighter pilots in Japan.
Although, unlike Yamamoto, whom he greatly admired,
he liked to drink a lot, he shared with the commander of
the Combined Fleet the realization of the importance of
the navy air force and the significance of aircraft carriers
in modern maritime warfare. As a result of his strategic
talent in navy aviation, he was subsequently entrusted
with pilot training.

After Fuchida, at Genda's instigation, was transferred to the aircraft carrier *Akagi*, where he had
served previously for a brief period, and given command in August 1941 of the navy flying squadrons,
he was initiated into the plans for Operation Hawaii
in September and entrusted with training the dive and
torpedo bomber squadrons for the secret mission. From
September, Japanese pilots underwent detailed training
for the attack on Pearl Harbor at the navy pilot bases on
Kyushu, the southernmost Japanese main island. While
dive bombers from the navy air force trained at the Usa
base in the north-east of Kyushu, the torpedo pilots
trained mainly in Kagoshima Bay.[24] The topography
of the coastal landscape before the volcano Sakurajima
was ideal for preparing for the attack on the US Pacific
Fleet, particularly on account of the depth of the bay
– 12 meters, almost identical to Pearl Harbor. Japan's
bomber pilots practiced both dive bombing and con-
ventional bombing from a great height, as well as the
precise altitude and timing for releasing the torpedoes.
While the horizontal bombers remained at high altitude,
the dive bombers were to descend as low as possible
over the surface of the water before releasing their torpedoes so as to ensure greater accuracy. The pilots soon
came up against a major problem in training, however.
The Model II torpedoes released from the air sank to
a depth of up to 20 meters (65 feet) in the water, with
the result that they would explode ineffectively in the

mud in the harbor basin, which was on average 12 meters deep and at its deepest point only 18 meters. This problem was ultimately solved by fitting the torpedoes with wooden fins. This gave them greater stability but also greater forward propulsion and prevented them from sinking lower than 12 meters, making them suitable for the attack on Pearl Harbor. The new technique and coordinated training significantly improved the accuracy of the bombers. After the Mitsubishi arms factory in Nagasaki had rapidly manufactured a sufficient number of these torpedoes, in mid-November Admiral Yamamoto now had his most important weapon for the attack available. The torpedoes were delivered to the *Kidō Butai* on November 17.[25]

The Kidō Butai *sets sail*

In late November 1941, no one on Hawaii had an inkling of the inferno that was to occur a few days later on the main island of Oahu. Because the war was raging in Europe and the continent was no longer a vacation destination, American tourism flourished in 1941 in the "Pacific paradise." A large number of military personnel had been transferred to Oahu with the Pacific Fleet. The sailors in their white uniforms were a common sight on the streets of the capital Honolulu and particularly in Pearl Harbor, where the US navy battleships were at anchor or in the shipyards. On Waikiki Beach, the main beach on the island, sailors mixed with tourists and inhabitants to enjoy their free time with their families or the local beauties. Duke Kahanamoku, an American Olympic swimmer born in Honolulu, had made surfing popular beyond Hawaii, and so not only locals but also US sailors sought to emulate the superstar known simply as the Big Kahuna (the big boss).[26] Thanks to the permanent presence of the fleet, Hawaii had become the most important US outpost in the Pacific. With its military airfields for the US army, the port facilities for the US navy, and the barracks and coastal batteries, the island of Oahu had become a veritable fortress.

On November 27, 1941, Chief of Naval Operations Admiral Harold R. Stark and army chief-of-staff George C. Marshall sent a general warning of a war with Japan to all US commanders in the Pacific. The US forces in Hawaii were also ordered to be particularly alert. The warnings did not mention Pearl Harbor specifically as a potential target of a Japanese attack, however.

In February 1941, Lieutenant-General Walter C. Short had been put in command of the 45,000 US army troops in Hawaii. He was ordered to protect Oahu, the main Hawaiian island, and the US Pacific Fleet in Pearl Harbor from attack by land or air. Different opinions were to be heard in the American high command in Hawaii as to the potential threat to the naval base in the Pacific if no diplomatic solution could be found to the tensions between the USA and Japan. Short did not expect an attack on the US naval base in the Pacific and failed to order any systematic radar monitoring. He was more afraid of acts of sabotage from among the 150,000 Japanese-Americans living on Hawaii – the largest ethnic group, accounting for 37 percent of the population.[27] When Admiral Stark warned again on November 27 of the danger of sabotage, Short, who suffered from a veritable "spy-itis" and "sabotage psychosis,"[28] reacted by ordering unusual measures. He had the aircraft stationed at Wheeler Field lined up in close formation in the middle of the airfield so they could be better guarded and protected from acts of sabotage. He rejected suggestions that the aircraft should be stored in bunkers to protect them from air raids. The airfield itself was not protected by trenches or any form of anti-aircraft fire. Despite this, Short, who saw his main task in Hawaii as training troops rather than taking defensive measures, believed that Pearl Harbor and the US Pacific Fleet were safe.

Admiral Husband E. Kimmel, commander-in-chief of the Pacific Fleet, known as a stickler for the rules and a fanatical defender of military discipline, had the aircraft carriers moved constantly in and out of the harbor – presumably to make it difficult for potential Japanese spies to predict the position of these valuable ships. He also ordered patrols by ships and navy aircraft and had all ships put in a state of alert in case of submarine attacks. After the warning of November 27, the American military leaders expected sabotage attacks or an advance by the Japanese fleet on Hawaii, but not an aerial attack.[29]

On November 29, Fukudome Shigeru, head of the department responsible for military operations and war strategy in the navy general staff in Tokyo, sent a message to the *Kidō Butai*, now in the north Pacific: "No hope for Japanese-American negotiations."[30] Vice Admiral Nagumo, commander of the "mobile force," drew the obvious conclusion: war between Japan and the USA. Was it too late? The Japanese government could have canceled the attack at the last moment and ordered the fleet to turn around. This was technically feasible, because although the *Kidō Butai* was underway in the north Pacific under radio silence and the radio stations on board had strict instructions not to send any messages, the channels for receiving signals from Tokyo remained open.[31]

On December 1 Japanese time, the *Kidō Butai* reached the International Date Line near the 180° line of longitude and entered the western hemisphere. In spite of the stormy weather, the ships were regularly refueled at sea. During the voyage, technicians on the aircraft carriers attached mountings for armor-piercing torpedoes to the Nakajima B5N aircraft. These last-minute modifications had not been made before departure because the attack preparations had taken place at short notice in view of the critical situation in Washington. Last-minute adjustments were also made to the twenty-one brand-new Zero fighters.[32]

"Climb Mount Niitaka 1208"[33] was the message signaled on December 2 to the *Kidō Butai* by the radio operator on the battleship *Nagato* at anchor on the island of Hashira in the bay south of Hiroshima. The order had been issued by Admiral Yamamoto, commander of the Combined Fleet. It was intended for Vice Admiral Nagumo as an indication to launch Operation Hawaii and the attack on Pearl Harbor. The number "1208" in the signal stood for the date of the attack, December 8, Japanese time, December 7 on Hawaii.

On December 3, wind speeds of 35 meters/second (126 km/h) made it impossible to refuel the ships at sea. The violent storm even swept a petty officer from the *Kaga* overboard. On December 4 Japanese time – a day earlier on Hawaii – at a position around 41°N 165°W, the *Kidō Butai* turned southward towards Hawaii. The storm abated the following day. Dense clouds covered the sky, and visibility was poor. The *Kidō Butai* also encountered a merchant ship. Had the fleet been discovered? The radio officers on the *Akagi* listened with bated breath to the radio traffic, but the merchant ship did not say anything about discovering Japanese warships. While the crew of the *Akagi* breathed a sigh of relief, the merchant ship disappeared over the horizon.

The following day, notices were posted on the ships saying: "The fate of the Empire depends on this campaign. Each one of you must do your utmost!"[34] This radio message sent a few hours previously came from Admiral Yamamoto himself as a last word of encouragement to the crews of the "mobile force." As on the flagship *Mikasa*, shortly before the Battle of Tsushima in 1905, a hammock was wrapped around the compass

of the *Sōryū* to protect it from shrapnel – as a clear
sign that the aircraft carrier was ready for action. At
Tsushima, the *Mikasa* had hoisted a Z signal flag to
indicate that a great battle was about to be engaged in.
Sailors now hoisted a Z flag on the mast of the *Akagi* as
a signal visible to everyone. A few minutes later the ships
of the *Kidō Butai* moved away from the seven refueling
ships, increased their speed to 24 knots (44.5 km/h), and
headed south to the agreed rendezvous 230 sea miles
(426 km) north of Pearl Harbor.[35]

Japanese spies on Hawaii

"Eight battleships in pairs moored in zone A, two aircraft carriers in zone B, ten heavy and three light cruisers,
and seventeen destroyers anchored in zone C; four light
and two heavy cruisers are just docking,"[36] reported
Yoshikawa Takeo to Tokyo from Honolulu on the morning of December 6. He was not the only spy on Hawaii.
Since September 1938, the German Bernhard Julius Otto
Kühn and his wife Ruth had been gathering information
about the US navy for the Japanese consulate general.
Until shortly before the Japanese attack they sent messages
to the navy general staff in Tokyo.[37] From 1941 the general staff also used its own military personnel for spying:
in March 1941, navy lieutenant Yoshikawa Takeo, who
already had detailed knowledge of the US navy, was sent
to Hawaii. Under the cover name Morimura Tadashi, he
pretended to be a local of Japanese origins and worked as
a driver, landscape gardener, or employee on US military
land or the private property of American officers in order
to obtain relevant information in this way. Kita Nagao,
the Japanese consul in Honolulu, sent this information
in code to the foreign ministry in Tokyo, which passed
it on to the navy general staff. The principal mission of
this local scout was to gather information on the posi-

tion of the US Pacific Fleet, the ship movements, airfields, defenses, and troop movements.

On May 12, 1941, Yoshikawa, who was to prove to be the most important of the Japanese spies, sent his first report with a list of the ships of the US Pacific Fleet at anchor. At first, he sent status reports about the American ships on the 10th of every month, but on November 15, with just under a month to go before the attack, he received the instruction from Tokyo to step up the information flow and report twice a week.[38] On December 2, the foreign ministry in Tokyo ordered the consulate in Honolulu to send daily reports.[39] Between May 12 and December 6, the day before the attack on Pearl Harbor, a total of 177 coded telegrams with information about the US Pacific Fleet were sent from Honolulu to Tokyo.[40] These reports, most of them from Yoshikawa, were passed on by the navy general staff to the headquarters of Admiral Yamamoto.

The Japanese war planners were quickly able to see that the US ships tended to go on maneuvers during the week but returned to anchor in Pearl Harbor at weekends. A third of the fleet was never in the harbor but on maneuvers on the high seas, although there was some overlap between the returning ships and those at anchor. As the planners had information not only about the maneuvers but also about the rest periods for the American crews and officers, they were able to determine the best day for a surprise attack, namely Sunday, December 7, 1941.

The espionage reports from Honolulu also indicated that the US battleships were not protected by a torpedo net. Given the increasingly critical situation in American-Japanese relations, however, the authorities in Tokyo expected a net to be installed in the near future, and at the Japanese naval base in Yokosuka, work proceeded feverishly – but ultimately unsuccessfully – to develop a torpedo that could penetrate such a net.[41]

To obtain local details and to plan the route of the *Kidō Butai* in the north Pacific, the officers Maejima, Matsuo, and Suzuki, members of navy intelligence, were also sent to Hawaii. Disguised as civilians, they traveled on the freight and passenger ship *Taiyō Maru* from the Nihon Yūsen Kaisha (NYK) line, which sailed from Yokohama on October 22. The route of the *Taiyō Maru*, which at this time transported Japanese living on Hawaii and Americans working in Japan, took it to the area around the latitude of 40°N, precisely where the *Kidō Butai* was also moving. During the voyage, the three officers took notes about the weather, the ships, and aircraft they encountered, and the possibilities for refueling the fleet. After the ship had arrived on Hawaii, the three officers met the Japanese consul, who sent their notes to Tokyo. They also obtained further information from locals with Japanese roots, including the fact that the US battleships were anchored in two rows in what was known as Battleship Row on Oahu south-east of Ford Island, while the anchorage at Lahaina in the north-west of the island of Maui was not in use. This information was particularly useful to the Japanese war planners as it had not been clear hitherto at which of the two Hawaiian anchorages the American battleships were located. It could now be assumed with great certainty that on the day of the planned attack they would be anchored off Ford Island.

After their return to Tokyo on November 17, the officers were summoned to the navy general staff to report on their spying activities in person. Officer Suzuki then proceeded to Kisarazu harbor in Chiba prefecture to board the *Hiei*, a battleship in the *Kidō Butai*. After Maejima and Matsuo had informed their fellow submariners at the Japanese base in Kure about the situation on Oahu, Matsuo boarded the submarine *I–22*, which also set off in the direction of Hawaii.[42]

The last information received directly before the start

of the attack on Pearl Harbor came not from the three Japanese officers but from Yoshikawa. In his message of the day before, December 6, he suggested that the US Pacific Fleet was unprepared for war and had not yet taken any specific defense measures. For example, there were no barrage balloons to make it more difficult for approaching aircraft to attack, with the result that the US ships were anchored without protection in the bay of Pearl Harbor – including two aircraft carriers and hence two of the main targets of the Japanese air force. Yoshikawa had in fact confused USS Utah with the targeted aircraft carrier USS Enterprise and incorrectly reported seeing a further carrier, probably USS Lexington, in the harbor.[43] From other spy reports, the navy general staff in Tokyo already knew that the Enterprise was no longer in Pearl Harbor in the first week of December, having set sail on December 3 with the two battleships USS Nevada and USS Oklahoma.[44] In subsequent reports, apart from the constant arrivals and departures of battleships, only one aircraft carrier, if any at all, was mentioned as being at anchor in Pearl Harbor.[45]

On the afternoon of December 6, Yoshikawa reported in his last telegram, no. 254, that the two aircraft carriers that had arrived in the harbor the previous evening and that he had reported that morning as being in zone B had just left the harbor with ten heavy cruisers. There were now not eight but nine battleships in Pearl Harbor. Yoshikawa seemed to include USS Utah, which he had mistaken that morning for an aircraft carrier. There were also seven light cruisers, nineteen destroyers, three submarine tenders, and many other vessels at anchor. The telegram clearly spoke of three submarine tenders, which he confirmed in his memoirs. Although often claimed in the research literature, there was never any mention of three aircraft carriers.[46] According to Yoshikawa's report, which

was sent from the consulate in Honolulu to the navy
general staff in Tokyo six hours before the attack, there
were no American aircraft carriers or heavy cruisers in
Pearl Harbor. The main targets of the Japanese attack
would not therefore be present during the first wave
of attack – a scenario that the war planners in Tokyo
should have taken much greater account of. The navy
general staff passed on this important information to
the commander of the *Kidō Butai*, which had been
provided with status reports from Honolulu on its way
to Hawaii since November 26. Yoshikawa's message
arrived on the *Akagi* three hours before the launch of
the first attack wave.[47]

According to the Japanese historian Akimoto Kenji,
the war planners in Tokyo were hoping to be able
to destroy at least four American aircraft carriers
during the attack, since the Japanese consulate had
passed on information to the navy general staff in mid-
November that the four aircraft carriers *Yorktown*,
Hornet, *Lexington*, and *Enterprise* were anchored in
Pearl Harbor – a report that proved retrospectively to
be incorrect. It was also possible, however, that *USS
Saratoga*, which was stationed in the Pacific as well,
would return to Pearl Harbor. Thus the Japanese navy
hoped that at least four aircraft carriers would be at
anchor when the attack was carried out. The Japanese
calculation was based on incorrect information, however: *USS Hornet*, launched from the naval shipyard
in Norfolk, Virginia, on the east coast of the USA, had
only been in service since the end of October. Like *USS
Yorktown* – which in mid-November had also been
reported incorrectly to be in Pearl Harbor – and the
aircraft carriers *Wasp* and *Ranger*, it was employed in
the Atlantic to escort conveys and protect them from
German submarine attacks. On the day of the attack
on Pearl Harbor, only three US aircraft carriers were
stationed in the Pacific. While *USS Saratoga* was in San

Diego on the west coast of the USA, *USS Lexington* had left Pearl Harbor on December 5 in the direction of Midway to reinforce the US air base established in the Pacific in 1940 with navy aircraft.[48] The closest aircraft carrier to Hawaii was *USS Enterprise*, which at the time of the Japanese attack was 215 sea miles (398 km) west of Pearl Harbor returning from Wake Island, where it had transported aircraft to reinforce the base there. Its return had been delayed because of a storm, and it was not expected to arrive in Pearl Harbor until the afternoon of December 7. It was illusory for the war planners in the Japanese navy, as Akimoto assumes, to have expected to sink four or five of the seven US aircraft carriers during the attack. To judge by the last message from Yoshikawa, however, it is more likely that the Japanese were aware that there were no aircraft carriers in Pearl Harbor. As Fuchida Mitsuo, commander of the first attack wave, stated after the war, Japan's air squadrons took off on the morning of December 7 in the vain hope, although they knew better, that Yoshikawa had been wrong and that perhaps there were aircraft carriers at anchor in Pearl Harbor after all, which would have made the attack even more worthwhile.[49] Moreover, shortly before the attack, the chief-of-staff and the commander of the *Kidō Butai*, Kusaka and Nagumo, appear to have been thinking more about their own aircraft carriers than the American ones. Nagumo feared that his fleet would be inferior to the US aircraft carriers and had received a strict order from the navy general staff not to lose a single carrier. The navy general staff was well aware that they would be barely sufficient to wage a war at sea in the Pacific, and for that reason great importance had been attached from the start of planning of the attack on Hawaii to ensuring the safety of the Japanese aircraft carriers. It is for that reason as well that Admiral Yamamoto had decided to concentrate six aircraft

carriers for the battle of Pearl Harbor – a revolutionary military strategy that would ensure a large number
of fighter aircraft and maximize the striking power
of the air force.[50] It would therefore appear that the
Japanese attack on December 7 was aimed less at the
(absent) aircraft carriers and more at the battleships in
the US Pacific Fleet, nine of which had been reported
by Yoshikawa to be at anchor on that Sunday morning.

The first encounter

"Whatever happens to me – if I go, it will be in the service of my country. Words cannot express how grateful
I am for the privilege of fighting for peace and justice."[51]
Sakamaki Kazuo laid down his pen in relief on the
morning of November 16, 1941. After careful consideration, the Japanese submariner felt confident that he
had found the right words for his farewell letter. The
twenty-two-year-old hoped that, if he died, patriotic
pride would fill his parents' hearts and comfort them for
the loss of their beloved son. The words of his superior
still rang in his ears. Shortly before Sakamaki wrote his
letter to his mother and father, Vice Admiral Shimizu
Mitsumi, commander of the 6th Fleet of submarines,
had read out to the crew the written order of the navy
general staff to prepare for war with the USA. Sakamaki
immediately suspected that he would probably soon
be sent on a mission with no return. Just a few weeks
earlier, he had been posted to a ten-man special unit
consisting of Kō-Hyōteki-class midget submarines (also
known as submarine-class type A). The smallest submarines, which had room for only a two-man crew, were
notable not only for their tiny size but above all for their
speed. Armed with two torpedoes at their bow, they
attained a speed of up to 24 knots (44.5 km/h) and were
the fastest of their type in the world. It was hoped that

the 24-meter-long and barely 2-meter-wide Kō-Hyōteki could be used to cause serious damage to or even sink large enemy battleships. The Japanese admiralty believed that victory over the US navy would depend on the surprise element but also on the tirelessly propagated greater willingness of their own troops to sacrifice themselves. If they had no other option, the submariners were to crash their midget submarines directly into the battleships, sacrificing their own lives in the process – kamikaze at sea!

From June 1941, Sakamaki and his comrades trained on the Japanese inland sea for the effective use of their submarines in a surprise attack. The recruits were told in late summer 1941 that possible targets would be the British bases in Hong Kong and Singapore and the American ports of San Francisco and Pearl Harbor. The submariners had studied the maps in great detail and were completely familiar with the layout of the harbors. The maneuvers on the north coast of the island of Shikoku, Sakamaki's home, also involved entering the bay through the narrow entrance to the harbor to simulate the channel leading to Pearl Bay on Oahu.

In early November 1941, five Kō-Hyōteki-class submarines were assembled to form the Third Submarine Squadron commanded by Lieutenant Iwasa Naoji. Submarine *HA-19* was commanded by Lieutenant Sakamaki Kazuo, with Inagaki Kiyoshi as his steersman. The tenders *I-16*, *I-18*, *I-20*, *I-22*, and *I-24* – 100-meter-long type I-16 submarines, each with a crew of around one hundred – were to transport the five Kō-Hyōteki-class midget submarines to Hawaii. The five submarines would be unloaded after sunset on the day before the attack 18 kilometers from the harbor entrance, from where they would penetrate secretly into the Pearl Harbor basin. They were to remain concealed in the bay and torpedo the American battleships following the first air raid. Once they had delivered their

130 kg torpedoes they were to secretly leave the harbor the same way they had entered it. The tenders would pick up the crews of the midget submarines, which were to be sunk, south of the Hawaiian island of Lanai, and return home with them.

After Sakamaki's submarine squadron had passed the US base on Wake Island without discovery, the five submarines entered Hawaiian waters as planned on December 5 and were able to tune in to the alien jazz music coming from the radio. Only a few hours later, Sakamaki discovered to his horror that the gyrocompass, the most important navigation instrument in his submarine, was defective. But this would not stop him from fulfilling his mission and, if necessary, giving his life for the Emperor. Even as a small boy, he had dreamed of serving his country as a soldier. As a teenager he had applied for admission to the navy academy, attracted by the esteem in which sailors were held after the Russo-Japanese War, not to mention the elegant uniform. In 1937, only one in twenty applicants was accepted, and Sakamaki Kazuo was one of them. Four years later his great moment to earn fame and honor had come. During his training, Sakamaki had learned absolute obedience and total willingness to sacrifice himself – characteristics that were meant to make Japanese soldiers superior to the well-equipped but spiritually and morally inferior Americans.

Inside submarine tender *I-24*, the last religious rites were performed to ritually cleanse body and soul. The submariners left not only letters to their families but also hair and fingernail cuttings so that their relatives would have something of their bodies to bury in the event that they died. If they failed to return from their mission, they would be enshrined as "war gods" in the Yasukuni Shrine to fallen Japanese soldiers. This would make their families very proud – a comforting thought for Sakamaki. In spite of the defective gyrocompass and the prospect of almost certain death, the lieutenant climbed with his steersman Inagaki into the midget submarine. An hour before midnight on December 6, the submarine tenders began to release the five Kō-Hyōteki submarines south-west of the entrance to Pearl Harbor. *HA-19* with Sakamaki on board was the last of the midget submarines to leave the tender *I-24*.

Because of the defective gyrocompass, *HA-19* was soon 90 degrees off course and was moving in a circle away from Pearl Harbor instead of heading towards the entrance to the harbor. In order to make his submarine capable in some way of maneuvering and to keep it on course as best he could, Sakamaki had no choice but to instruct his steersman to keep at periscope depth and at low speed. According to the plan, all five submarines should be in the harbor by dawn and hide near the seabed. But Sakamaki's circling submarine was still far outside the harbor. The island of Oahu could be clearly made out through the periscope, along with two American ships patrolling the entrance to the harbor. Sakamaki told his companion Inagaki resolutely: "Have no fear. We have come so far and it is our duty to fulfill our mission. Somehow we will get past the patrols and penetrate into the harbor. As soon as we are inside, we will surface. Then we will fire our torpedoes at a battleship and, if necessary, ram it. That is our mission! In a few hours our fate will be sealed. Chin up!" Like their comrades in the sister submarines, the crew of the *HA-19* were determined to fulfill their mission of destruction.[52]

Just before 4 a.m. on the night of December 6 to 7, the thirty-five-year-old commander of the destroyer *USS Ward*, Lieutenant William Outerbridge, received a radio signal. The minesweepers *USS Condor* and *USS Crossbill*, which were patrolling that night just a few sea miles south of the entrance to Pearl Harbor, had spotted a submarine periscope sticking out of the water. Outerbridge, who had only taken command of

USS Ward on December 5, immediately put his crew on alert and scanned the area with an echo depth sounder, albeit without success. He abandoned the search around 4.30 a.m. The highest alarm level, red alarm, on the *USS Ward* was canceled. Half an hour later the patrol boats *USS Condor* and *USS Crossbill* returned to their anchorages in Pearl Harbor. To allow the two minesweepers to enter the harbor, a section of the net placed across the harbor to keep out enemy submarines was lifted. It was to remain open until 8.40 a.m.[53]

At around 6.30 a.m., *USS Ward*, which was still patrolling at the entrance to the harbor, received another radio signal. A reconnaissance plane and the maintenance ship *USS Antares*, which was towing a barge to Pearl Harbor, had made another suspicious discovery. A submarine appeared to be attempting to enter the harbor unobserved in the wake of the *Antares*. When the *Ward* arrived, one of the reconnaissance planes sent from Pearl Harbor, a Consolidated PBY Catalina, had already gone in pursuit of the submarine, one of the Japanese midget submarines from the *I-16* tender, with comrades of Sakamaki on board. At around 6.45 a.m., like the two-engine Catalina, the *Ward* also began to drop depth charges. Soon an oil slick rose to the surface, indicating that at least one of the four depth charges had hit its target. The *Ward* had sunk the midget submarine. Shortly before 7 a.m., Lieutenant Outerbridge reported to the Pearl Harbor naval base that an enemy submarine had been sunk at the harbor entrance. This news should have acted as a warning to the personnel responsible for opening and closing the net and protecting the entrance to the harbor, not to mention to Admiral Husband E. Kimmel, commander-in-chief of the Pacific Fleet. But neither Kimmel, who did not receive the information until 7.30 a.m., nor his officers gave much credence to the report. There had often been reports of this nature in the past that had proved to be false alarms. Outerbridge's report was thus ignored and not passed on to the US army and its commander on Hawaii, Lieutenant-General Walter C. Short, nor was the US navy put on alert. Even years after the war, Outerbridge's report on the sinking of a submarine was rejected as being unrealistic. It was not until the discovery of the wreck of a midget submarine by a Hawaiian research team in 2002, a few kilometers from Pearl Harbor, that Outerbridge's narration of the events was confirmed, decades later. In the early morning of December 7, the USS Ward had killed the crew of the Japanese midget submarine with its depth charges and accounted for the first deaths. They were not to be the last.[54]

3

The Attack

The first wave

In the dawn twilight at around 5.30 a.m., the heavy cruisers *Tone* and *Chikuma*, part of the *Kidō Butai*, each sent a reconnaissance plane to Hawaii.[1] One of the two planes flew in the direction of Pearl Harbor, the other to the second-largest anchorage on the island of Maui south-east of Oahu, the deep-water Lahaina harbor, to determine whether and where the US warships were anchored. Directly before the attack, information on the precise location of the fleet, the defenses, and the cloud cover and wind direction was absolutely essential. As the entrance to the harbor was difficult to access, the view through a periscope imprecise, and the danger of discovery great, the commander of the "mobile force," Vice Admiral Nagumo, had preferred not to use submarines for reconnaissance but to send the two planes instead.

Meanwhile, the pilots in the first attack wave were making their final preparations on the aircraft carriers. The crew of the flagship *Akagi* gave Fuchida Mitsuo a *hachimaki*, a traditional headband with the inscription "determined to win," which was meant to bring luck and strength. Visibly moved, the commander of the first attack wave tied the *hachimaki* around his head and got ready to take off. Shortly afterwards, 183 planes took off together from all six aircraft carriers. Only two planes intended for the first wave remained behind. One crashed on takeoff – the pilot was rescued – and the second had engine damage and failed to take off at all from the *Kaga*. Around 6.30 a.m. the fighters and bombers led by Fuchida maneuvered into a V formation for the flight of 230 sea miles (426 km) south-westward to Hawaii.[2]

Harada Kaname was one of the pilots to take off from the *Sōryū* over the Pacific in his Zero on this early morning. He was an experienced fighter pilot who had taken part in numerous air battles during the Second Sino-Japanese War. "In case the enemy attacks, we need experienced airmen like you to protect the fleet,"[3] his squadron leader had told him. Disappointed, the twenty-five-year-old fighter pilot looked down at his comrades in the first attack wave. As an escort, he was responsible for securing the airspace over the "mobile force" and could not accompany the attackers.[4]

More than 200 sea miles (370 km) west of Oahu, a reconnaissance squadron of eighteen Douglas SBD Dauntless dive bombers took off at around the same time as the Japanese planes. They formed the vanguard of the aircraft carrier *USS Enterprise*, which was returning to Hawaii from the Wake Island base.

When Fuchida's pilots had covered around half the distance to Pearl Harbor, a warning was sounded at Opana Ridge, the US army radar station on the north coast of Oahu. In view of the strong echo on the radar screen, the two operators, George Elliot and Joseph Lockard, assumed that a huge fleet of aircraft was approaching. Without delay, they reported to the army headquarters at Fort Shafter in the south of Oahu. Fatefully, however, the entire signals platoon was at breakfast. Only Lieutenant Kermit Tyler, who was on just his second duty spell at the radar control and was inexperienced

at assessing reports of this nature, was present. "It was
the largest group I'd ever seen [on the radar]. It looked
. . . like a main pulse,"[5] Lockard had told him excit-
edly on the phone, without saying how many planes
were involved. Tyler therefore misinterpreted the report
from Opana Ridge and said comfortingly to Lockard:
"OK. It's all right."[6] Tyler assumed that it was a B-17
bomber squadron that had set off from the US mainland and was expected in Hawaii in the morning of
December 7. Elliot and Lockard continued to observe
the radar screen until 7.40 a.m., when the echoes from
the approaching Japanese armada became lost in the
background interference. Shortly before 8 a.m., they
left the radar room for breakfast.[7]

Around 7.40 a.m., the reconnaissance plane that had
taken off from the *Chikuma* reported that there were
nine battleships at anchor in Pearl Harbor, as well
as one heavy and six light cruisers. The pilot said the
weather was good with a clear view of the US Pacific
Fleet – important information for Fuchida's approaching first wave. "No enemy ships in Lahaina,"[8] reported
the pilot of the reconnaissance plane that had taken
off from the heavy cruiser *Tone*. For Fuchida's pilots,
this meant that the attack would concentrate on Pearl
Harbor. They would have turned back at the last
moment only if they had received negative reports from
the reconnaissance planes. While the *Chikuma* plane
returned to the *Kidō Butai*, the second plane made a further tour to the south to look out for American aircraft
carriers. As the USS *Enterprise* was moving towards
Hawaii from the west, however, the only aircraft carrier
near the island remained undetected.

A few minutes after the pilots in the first attack wave
broke through the cloud cover, they saw the outline of
the north coast of Oahu. Fuchida was relieved: as the
scouts had announced, the visibility on this December
morning was good – perfect conditions for an attack.

He noted as well with relief that there were no enemy aircraft to be seen anywhere in the sky. He fired his Very pistol to signal his bombers to be ready for the attack. As he could not be sure that everyone had seen the signal, he fired a second flare. Lieutenant-Commander Takahashi Kakuichi, who was in command of the dive bomber squadrons on the two Crane-class aircraft carriers *Zuikaku* and *Shōkaku*, saw both flares, and because he misinterpreted the second signal, he gave his Aichi D3A formation the immediate order to dive and attack. Murata Shigeharu, who commanded the main torpedo bomber squadron from the *Akagi*, saw immediately that Fuchida's signal had been misinterpreted. The commander of the first attack wave had great respect for Murata, who had become famous in the late 1930s as an ace bomber in the skies over China. He was nicknamed "Boots" by his comrades in training on account of his distinctive footwear. Later on, Fuchida and other fellow airmen changed this nickname to "Butsu" (Buddha, saint) on account of his military prowess. As Butsu could no longer intervene and stop Takahashi from attacking, he also had his torpedo bomber squadron prepare to attack. Fuchida was annoyed for a moment at the premature and unauthorized action by his bombers, but he also realized that it would no longer make much difference. He was sure that the US Pacific Fleet was not expecting the attack and that the surprise element would succeed. At 7.49 a.m., eleven minutes before the planned start of the attack, Fuchida therefore radioed the words "to, to, to," short for *totsugeki*, "attack!" The assault could now begin.[9]

"Tora Tora Tora"

In the early morning of December 7, the attorney Ray Buduick took off from Oahu in his small powered

aircraft to show his seventeen-year-old son Martin
the island from above. He unexpectedly encountered
aircraft in his path with a red sun as marking. They
were Japanese Zeros, which opened fire without warning. Buduick took fright and headed back to Honolulu,
where he managed to land in spite of slight damage
to his plane. This was the first engagement between a
Japanese fighter plane and an American civilian aircraft
in the skies over Hawaii.[10]

Just a few moments after this first encounter, over
Oahu, the Nakajima B5N torpedo bombers, called
"Kate" by the Americans, attacked Pearl Harbor in
two lines. Two squadrons, each with eight aircraft,
commanded by squadron leaders Matsumura and
Nagai from the Dragon-class aircraft carriers *Hiryū*
and *Sōryū*, approached Ford Island from the north-
west. The second line, with two squadrons of bombers
from the *Akagi* and *Kaga* led by Murata and Kitajima,
headed south over Hickam Field military airfield, and
descended towards the American battleships anchored
in Battleship Row.

At 7.50 a.m., twenty-five dive bombers from the
Zuikaku, escorted by eight Zero fighters, arrived at
Wheeler Field airfield, practically in the center of Oahu.
The rapid destruction of the US army aircraft stationed
there was essential for the success of the Japanese mission, as this was the only way of preventing an American
counterattack on the Japanese aircraft carriers. The
eight Zeros, commanded by Lieutenant Suganami from
the *Sōryū*, first buzzed over Wheeler Field. The new
fighter aircraft had only recently had their baptism of
fire in September over the skies of Chungking in China.
The rapid and agile aircraft strafed the American planes
with machine guns. By order of Lieutenant-General
Walter C. Short, the planes had been grouped on the
runways to prevent sabotage and were thus an easy
target. Suganami and his comrades also hailed machine

gun fire on the administrative buildings and crew quarters. Then the dive bombers released their payloads on Wheeler Field. Most of the US Army Air Force fighters – outmoded Curtiss P-36 and P-40 Tomahawks – were destroyed on the ground. The Zero fighters then homed in again on the US planes and hangars, some of which caught fire. Kerosene leaked from some of the riddled aircraft on the ground, and as the planes were closely grouped, the fire quickly spread from one to another. US soldiers desperately attempted to roll some of the still intact planes from the runway so as at least to limit the damage. Meanwhile the Zeros came in to attack Wheeler Field again.

At 7.53 a.m., six of the Zeros from the *Hiryū*, led by Lieutenant Okajima, which had acted as escort on the way to Pearl Harbor, headed for the Ewa Mooring Mast Field airfield in the south-west of Oahu to attack the forty-eight planes from US Marine Air Group 21. At the same time, eleven Mitsubishi A6M fighters from the *Shōkaku* and *Zuikaku* attacked Kaneohe Bay Naval Air Station in the north-east of the island.

Important US military airfields on Oahu were now under attack by the Japanese. The surprise had been perfect. Fuchida radioed the signal "Tora Tora Tora," the Japanese word for "tiger," to the *Kidō Butai*. It stood for *totsugeki raigeki* (lightning attack) and indicated that the attack on the unsuspecting enemy had been a total success. Like a tiger jumping out to ambush its prey, the Japanese assailants on this Sunday morning, December 7, had taken the most important US military base in the Pacific completely by surprise.

In the meantime, Suganami's fighter squadron had also reached the airspace above Ewa Mooring Mast Field. As in the attack on Wheeler Field, the Zeros swooped down three times and strafed the undefended fighters. The victims this time were reconnaissance bombers and Wildcat type F4F American navy fighters,

Planes and hangars wrecked in the Japanese attack on
Pearl Harbor.
Courtesy National Archives, photo no. 12009004

some of which had arrived in the Pacific from the
Grumman factory in New York only a few weeks
earlier. The sole return fire came from a machine gun
hurriedly mounted on the wing of a reconnaissance
aircraft on the ground. The defenders of Ewa Mooring
Mast Field managed in this way to shoot down at least

one Zero. In total, however, the attack was devastating for the Americans, and all forty-eight aircraft stationed at the airfield were put out of action. It had taken only a few minutes to completely destroy everything.

The defenders of the Kaneohe Bay Naval Air Station, commanded by Harold M. Martin, suffered a similar fate. Within ten minutes, the Catalinas, two-engine patrol bombers used above all for reconnaissance and therefore a great danger for the Japanese fleet, were destroyed on the ground. The only fire truck was also hit and could not be used. Anti-aircraft batteries that should have been installed on the naval base had been fatefully transferred just two days earlier to the army bases.[11]

Just before 8 a.m., the aircraft in the first attack wave also reached their primary target, Pearl Harbor and the small Ford Island off it, and Hickam Field airfield, named for the US air force pioneer Lieutenant-Colonel Horace M. Hickam, where the US bombers were stationed.

Lieutenant-Commander Logan Ramsey arrived at the command headquarters of Ford Island Naval Air Station just before 8 a.m. He had been informed half an hour earlier that a Catalina had spotted a submarine while patrolling the entrance to Pearl Harbor, which had been sunk shortly afterwards. Ramsey believed that at this early hour it could only have been an exercise – or else a false alarm. It did not occur to him that it was the prelude to a real attack on the base. Everything that Sunday morning had been completely normal, and the crews had been having their breakfast in their messes. While some of the soldiers were preparing to go on duty, others were getting ready for church to celebrate the second Sunday in Advent. Many were looking forward to seeing their families again over Christmas and the New Year. Even though Ramsey did not believe in the slightest that there was any danger, he dutifully wrote a report for the commander of the Pacific Fleet, Admiral Kimmel, on the submarine incident. He now waited for confirmation in the command center. When he looked out of the window, a single plane crossed his field of vision. A few seconds later it swooped down over Ford Island. Low-level flying was not allowed, but Ramsey assumed that it was an inexperienced young pilot who had not realized that his maneuver violated the flight safety of Pearl Harbor. The plane ascended again and flew off. While Ramsey was wondering how he could identify the plane, his thoughts were interrupted by a loud explosion. The unidentified plane must have dropped a torpedo: Pearl Harbor was being attacked. Ramsey ran down the corridor to the radio room to sound the alarm on all channels on the base: "Air raid, Pearl Harbor! This is NOT a drill!"[12] A few minutes later, the radio station KGMB interrupted its music program to announce "All army, navy, and marine personnel, report to duty!"[13] Two further messages of this nature were broadcast in the following twenty minutes.

In the meantime, Matsumura's torpedo bomber squadron had reached its destination. Three ships lay at anchor north-west of Ford Island, one of which the squadron leader identified as *USS Utah*. This Florida-class battleship had been launched in 1909 and was now used solely as a US navy training vessel and was no longer intended for battle. It had carried out air defense exercises in the Hawaiian waters before being anchored in the bay. Like the nearby light cruisers *USS Detroit*, *USS Raleigh*, and *USS Tangier*, the *Utah* was of secondary importance for the Japanese attackers. The torpedo bombers had been given strict instructions to reserve their torpedoes for the large battleships and aircraft carriers. Matsumura therefore ordered his squadron to turn round to seek more worthwhile targets. Unlike Matsumura's pilots, however, six torpedo bombers from the squadron led by Nagai swooped

down on the *Utah* and *Raleigh* – named for the capital
of the US state of North Carolina. They dropped their
torpedoes, and a short while afterwards loud explosions
were to be heard, whose shockwaves were felt even by
the Japanese pilots in their planes. Water spurted up like
a geyser from around the four ships. The spray soaked
the clothing of the surprised sailors on the deck of the
Raleigh. They hastily manned the anti-aircraft turrets to
fire at the attackers. No sooner had the first rounds been
fired, however, than the ship began to list to port. A torpedo had evidently hit the light cruiser. Masses of water
flooded inside the ship. The crew attempted to prevent
it from capsizing by counter-flooding and jettisoning
all heavy objects, such as the derrick and torpedo tubes
and ammunition. They ultimately succeeded. *USS Utah*,
which Matsumura had wanted to spare, was hit by two
torpedoes. An inexperienced and over-enthusiastic pilot
from Matsumura's squadron had opened fire on the
ship, which now began slowly to sink. After ten minutes
it capsized. Some of the crew managed to get to the
Tangier, anchored behind it, which returned fire. Many
members of the crew of the *Utah* lost their lives in Pearl
Harbor, however: six of the thirty-six officers and fifty-
eight of the 498 sailors.[14]

Nagai meanwhile continued flying. He thought he
spotted a battleship in the shipyard on Ten Ten Pier
in the south of Ford Island. It must have been *USS
Pennsylvania*, which according to Japanese intelligence
was usually at anchor here. Believing he had found an
ideal target, he began to drop his torpedo. In fact it was
not a battleship but *USS Oglala*, a minelayer, named for
a Sioux tribe. As it had a shallower draught than larger
battleships, the torpedo raced underneath the hull and
hit the starboard side of the light cruiser *USS Helena*,
which was anchored next to it. While the crew of the
Helena successfully prevented their ship from capsizing, the *Oglala*, which had not been hit, began to sink.

The *USS Oglala* capsized and sinking.
Courtesy National Archives, photo no. 12009013

What had happened? The enormous pressure from the torpedo impact on the *Helena* had caused the *Oglala*'s wooden hull to burst. The flagship minelayer capsized in the direction of the harbor and threatened to push the *Helena* up against the dock. Admiral Furlong, commander of the navy shipyard, was quick-witted enough to see the impending danger and ordered the *Oglala* to be towed away so as to save the *Helena* at least. By 9.30 a.m. the *Oglala* had listed so far to starboard that it was no longer possible to stand upright on deck. It had to be left, and it capsized a few minutes after the crew had been ordered by Furlong to abandon ship.[15]

Battleship Row in crossfire

As the spy Yoshikawa had said in his last report sent from Honolulu, there were nine ships anchored in pairs in Battleship Row in the south-east of Ford Island. The Japanese attackers thought incorrectly that all nine battleships in the US Pacific Fleet were to be found there, but *USS Pennsylvania* was in dry dock and *USS Colorado* had been transferred to Bremerton, Washington, for repair. Apart from the seven battleships *Arizona*, *California*, *Maryland*, *Nevada*, *Oklahoma*, *Tennessee*, and *West Virginia*, the tanker *Neosho* and the repair ship *Vestal* were moored there.

The torpedo bombers from the *Akagi* and *Kaga* led by ace bomber Murata reached Battleship Row before 8 a.m. When sailors on the *USS Vestal* saw the approaching bomber squadron, they immediately sounded the alarm and opened fire on the attackers. The first torpedo from a bomber in Murata's squadron hit the sea-facing *Oklahoma*. South-west of the ship at the tip of Battleship Row was the *California*, a heavily armored Tennessee-class battleship. Its crew attempted to escape the inferno and to set off to sea. The ship was hit hard by two torpedoes and threatened to capsize. Shortly afterwards it was rocked by a bomb, which hit the ammunition chamber, setting the ship on fire.

The *Oklahoma* also received serious hits. It was anchored to the port of the *Maryland* on the outside of the anchorage and was therefore an easy target. After the first three torpedo hits, it began slowly to list.

Captain Howard D. Bode had left the ship at 7.30 a.m.
and was on board the neighboring *Maryland* for the
Sunday service. First Officer J. L. Kenworthy was left
in charge of the *Oklahoma*. Before he could do anything to prevent the ship capsizing, it was hit by five
more torpedoes. Just twenty minutes after the start of
the attack, the huge Nevada-class ship was lying on its
side. Sailors jumped overboard or clambered in despair
up to the part of the ship that was not yet submerged
in the hope of being rescued. Some of them were taken
on board the *Maryland*, which was already firing back
at the oncoming planes. When a ninth torpedo hit the
Oklahoma, it continued to turn to port and began to
sink head-first, its keel pointing upwards. Because Pearl
Harbor was not particularly deep – just 12 meters on
average – the US military authorities had thought that
the ships of the Pacific Fleet would be safe from torpedo attacks – a disastrous miscalculation. The torpedo
attack on the *Oklahoma* cost the lives of 429 crew
members.[16]

At the end of Battleship Row was the *Oklahoma*'s
sister ship the *Nevada*. Like the other battleships, it
came under fire shortly after 8 a.m. The anti-aircraft
batteries on the 180-meter-long Nevada-class battleship responded to the attack, as the crew attempted
desperately to keep the Japanese planes at bay. One of
the torpedo bombers was indeed hit and crashed down
in flames, but the pilot still managed to release his payload. His torpedo penetrated the ship's hull, and huge
amounts of water flooded into the *Nevada*'s hold. First
Officer Francis J. Thomas had the bulkheads closed and
counter-flooded to prevent the ship from listing.[17]

The ship worst hit on Battleship Row, however, was
the Pennsylvania-class *Arizona*, thought to be unsink-
able. After an 800 kg bomb had penetrated its armor
and caused a huge explosion in the main ammunition
chamber, it sank like a stone to the bottom of the bay.

In less than ten minutes, the *Arizona*, which had joined the Pacific Fleet twenty years earlier, was gone. Hit by two bombs, it took with it over 1,100 sailors – almost half of the losses incurred by the Americans in the attack on Pearl Harbor.[18]

A burning oil slick spread from the seriously hit and sinking *Arizona*, which also threatened the *Nevada* anchored behind it. The latter's First Officer, Francis J. Thomas, realized that his ship needed to get out of the danger zone as quickly as possible to escape the inferno on the water and the bombers in the air. The ship, which had been part of the Pacific Fleet for ten years, was fortunately more easily maneuverable

Japanese aerial photo of the first attack wave, showing Ford Island, the US battleships anchored on Battleship Row, and a huge spout of water caused by torpedo detonation.
Private Collection Peter Newark Military Pictures/Bridgeman Images

because it was anchored alone, unlike the other ships in Battleship Row, which were in pairs. A short time later, the *Nevada*, one of the first US navy ships to be fitted with triple gun turrets, was heading at full steam for the entrance to the harbor.

Next to the *Arizona*, facing the sea, was *USS Vestal*, and the burning oil slick threatened to set it on fire. Two bombs intended for the *Arizona* hit the *Vestal*, which soon began to list. At 8.10 a.m., a further torpedo penetrated the starboard side of the *Arizona* close to the second gun turret. It was a direct hit on the powder magazine and ammunition chamber, causing a massive explosion in the bow of the ship. The shockwave caught the crew members on the deck of the *Vestal* and swept them into the water. Among the sailors thrown overboard was the ship's captain Cassin Young. He managed to swim through the oil slick back to his ship, which was now also in flames.[19]

While the burning oil slick around the *Arizona* threatened the ships anchored at the back end of Battleship Row, there were worries at the front end that the 25,000-ton fleet tanker *USS Neosho* would explode, since it contained not oil but high-octane and hence particularly reactive aircraft fuel. Fortunately, the dockside tanks had been filled from the *Neosho* only minutes before the attack, but the captain still tried to remove his ship from the anchorage. Like the *Nevada*, the *Neosho* managed to escape the inferno thanks to its exposed position at the end of the anchorage. Around three-quarters of an hour after the start of the attack, the tanker sailed westward towards the nearby Southeast Loch bay. It docked at Merry's Point at 9.30 a.m.[20]

At about the same time as the *Oklahoma* was hit for the first time, a torpedo from Murata's Nakajima B5N squadron also hit *USS West Virginia*, which was sea-side parallel to *USS Tennessee*. A Colorado-class battleship, its powerful, long-range 16-inch guns made it the most modern warship in the US navy, with heavy armor to protect it from mines and torpedoes. Because of its position, however, it now offered an easy target for the torpedoes dropped into the bay. After it had been hit twice, it began to list in the direction of the harbor. A further seven torpedoes and two bombs caused the ship to be enshrouded in black smoke, and it threatened to sink.

One of the crew members of the *West Virginia* was perhaps the most unusual American war hero of Pearl Harbor. When the ship came under fire, the African-American Doris "Dorie" Miller from Texas, also known on board as a heavyweight boxer, rushed to the anti-aircraft guns. The remarkable thing is that Miller was not a trained machine gun operator but a cook. He continued shooting until the ammunition ran out, then looked after the wounded. They included the captain, Mervyn Sharp Bennion, severely injured by the shrapnel from an explosion on the neighboring *USS Tennessee*, who died on board from his wounds. In May 1942, Miller became the first African-American to receive the Navy Cross, the highest award given by the US navy. As prejudice against Blacks was still widespread in the US armed forces at the start of the war, Miller became a symbolic figure in the African-American community and the personification of their contribution to the war. Like so many of his comrades on the *West Virginia*, however, he did not live to see the end of the war: he was killed on November 24, 1943, in the Battle of Tawara in the Gilbert Islands.[21]

Apart from the battleships on Battleship Row, the Japanese attackers also targeted Ford Island itself. The hangars, seaplane docking areas, and most of the aircraft themselves were soon in flames. As at Wheeler Field, the American pilots on Ford Island tried to wheel the few undamaged aircraft away from those that were burning.

Doris "Dorie" Miller was celebrated in the American press – as in this cartoon – for his heroism in firing at attacking Japanese aircraft.
Courtesy National Archives, photo no. 208-COM-43

While the Japanese were attacking Battleship Row and Ford Island, some American torpedo boats in the naval shipyard south-east of the island were being prepared for transportation to the US base on the Philippines on board the oil tanker *Ramapo*. The crew of one of the torpedo boats hurried to the gun turret and opened fire on the attackers.[22] One burst of machine gun fire hit a Japanese aircraft which plummeted into the sea. The sailors on the other torpedo boats also wanted to open fire but their boats were in the process of being loaded and were suspended in the air at the side of the oil tanker. Because the engines had been turned off for transport, the sailors had to muscle the turrets into the right position for them to be used at all.[23]

As Fuchida's planes were attacking Battleship Row, the reconnaissance planes from the aircraft carrier *USS Enterprise* arrived at Oahu, which had now become a battlefield. The pilots of the eighteen Douglas SBD Dauntless bombers were taken completely by surprise by what they saw. They had to deal right away with the Japanese fighters. The Zeros from the *Akagi* led by Lieutenant-Commander Itaya fitted with 20 mm guns in their wings shot down four SBDs, and a fifth was hit by a Japanese dive bomber and crashed. The sailors on the vessels in Battleship Row had manned the anti-aircraft batteries on board to fight back with desperate courage against the attackers. As it was impossible for them to distinguish friend from foe, a further plane from the *Enterprise* reconnaissance squadron was downed by friendly fire.[24]

Aircraft also approached the island from the north-east: twelve unarmed B-17 bombers, better known as Flying Fortresses. They were the machines that had taken off from California and were expected in Hawaii in the morning of December 7. When the Opana Ridge radar station reported the approaching Japanese attackers, Kermit Tyler, the duty officer in the radar room at the army headquarters in Fort Shafter, had mistakenly assumed that they were the bomber squadron. When some of the pilots now attempted to land their aircraft on Hickam Field in the south of the bay of Pearl Harbor – the most important airfield in Hawaii and home of the 18th Bombardment Wing and the 5th and 11th Heavy Bombardment Groups – they couldn't believe their eyes. Five minutes after the attack on Wheeler Field in the center of Oahu, the first wave of attackers had turned their attention to Hickam Field, and the Zeros fired on the US bombers on the ground in the same way they had done at Wheeler. Most of the planes were two-engine Douglas B-18s, but there were also twelve modern B-17 Flying Fortresses. Many aircraft and hangars were in flames. The B-17 bombers from California, which were on their way to the Philippines and were meant only to stop and refuel on Hawaii, were also attacked by the Japanese fighters. They attempted desperately to land at Hickam Field or somewhere else on Oahu. In the highly chaotic situation, the arrival of the B-17s from the American mainland also caused confusion among the defenders of Hickam Field. The only Flying Fortresses on Hawaii were of type B-17D, and many of those present, such as fighter pilot Major Brooke E. Allen, had never before seen the new B-17E. Allen, who knew nothing of the arrival from California, thought at first: "Where did the Japs get four-engine bombers?"[25] It was only minutes later, when some of the bombers were already under fire, that he realized the US soldiers were shooting at their own planes. The damage caused by this friendly fire was much less than that inflicted by the Japanese fighters, however. After the attack on Hickam Field, more than half of the fifty-five bombers on the ground had been destroyed or put out of action.[26]

Shortly after the start of the attack on Hickam Field, American soldiers in Fort Kamehameha to the south rushed to their machine gun posts. Like the anti-aircraft guns on the destroyer *USS Helm* – the only ship that was moving within Pearl Harbor when the attack started – the machine guns took aim at the approaching Zeros. One aircraft from Itaya's squadron was hit and crashed not far from Fort Kamehameha.

Within half an hour of the start of the first Japanese attack, the vessels on Battleship Row were in flames or on the verge of sinking, and the American fighters and bombers had been destroyed on the ground at the airfields before they could even take off. The fire trucks

had now arrived at the burning main airfield Hickam
Field and were attempting to extinguish the flames,
but they were under constant attack from low-flying
Japanese fighters. Some firemen were killed. Locals
from Pearl City, Honolulu, and the surrounding area
had rushed to witness the surreal spectacle. Among the
eyewitnesses were Japanese-Americans from Oahu, who
were American citizens but with Japanese ancestors.
Very few of the observers realized what was happening. While passengers on a liner from San Francisco
believed they were witnessing a spectacular maneuver,
others were convinced that a terrible accident had taken
place and that oil tanks in the harbor had exploded.
They regarded the events with disbelief.[27] The American
sailors on the ships in Battleship Row quickly realized
that they had been the victims of an underhand surprise
attack. Many of their comrades had been killed almost
immediately. The battleships were heavily damaged and
on fire and were on the verge of sinking. A burning oil
slick was spreading over the harbor with debris and
injured and lifeless bodies floating in it. The moans and
screams of the wounded mingled with the salvos fired
from the attacking aircraft and the uncoordinated anti-
aircraft gunfire.

Among the observers of this terrible spectacle was
Admiral Husband E. Kimmel, commander-in-chief of
the Pacific Fleet. He had left his quarters at the naval
shipyard shortly after the start of the attack and was
driving to the headquarters. From here he could see
the entire harbor and follow the unending attacks by
Japanese bombers on his warships. If he turned away
from Battleship Row and looked south, the view was
no more comforting. Japanese aircraft were circling
like vultures over their prey at Hickam Field, from
which thick swathes of black smoke could be seen. At
8.12 a.m., Kimmel reported to Washington: "Hostilities
with Japan commenced with air raid on Pearl Harbor."[28]

While Kimmel was watching helplessly at the window as the attacks continued ceaselessly, there was suddenly a loud noise. Kimmel took a few steps backwards, bent down and picked up a spent .50 caliber bullet. It came from a machine gun and had penetrated the window-pane and hit the fifty-nine-year-old admiral in the chest. While the attack on Pearl Harbor, Kimmel's most tragic hour, was to remain in the American collective memory as a great military defeat, the bullet had miraculously left only a small black spot on the admiral's gleaming white uniform.[29]

While Kimmel watched in shock as the scenario played out before his eyes, for the sailors of the US navy a small glimmer of hope was discerned on the horizon in this dramatic hour. One of the ships – the destroyer *USS Helm* – had escaped the inferno and sailed at full speed through the channel in West Loch to safety on the open sea. At 8.17 a.m., shortly after the *Helm* had left the harbor, the crew spotted a stranded submarine. The midget submarine *HA-19* commanded by Sakamaki Kazuo had had great difficulty approaching the entrance to Pearl Harbor that morning. Because of the defective gyrocompass it had become almost impossible to maneu-ver, and the vessel had run aground on a coral reef and was now stranded. The *Helm* opened fire on the sub-marine. A loud explosion was heard inside it, shaking it to the core. Sakamaki lost consciousness for a moment, and when he came round he saw white smoke, but the shots from the *Helm* had in fact missed their target and freed the submarine. Inagaki had the presence of mind to immediately put the engines into reverse and steer the submarine back into the water at full speed. The fire from the *Helm* or the coral reef had damaged the torpedo and made it unusable, however. Even more dan-gerous was the fact that the battery had been hit and was giving off toxic fumes. The two-man crew began to feel lightheaded on account of the lack of oxygen and were in life-threatening danger. Without a usable weapon or the ability to maneuver, the hunter had become the hunted. Sakamaki ordered his steersman, despite the defective gyrocompass, to attempt evasive action and to head for the island of Lanai, one of the eight main Hawaiian islands, where it was to rendezvous with the submarine tender. The submarine managed to get away from the *Helm*, but it drifted for hours in the water, badly damaged and incapable of maneuvering with two dazed seamen on board, before finally running aground. After Sakamaki and Inagaki had activated the self-destruct mechanism, they left the vessel and attempted with their last strength to reach land. They realized on the way that they had not heard an explosion and that the self-destruct mechanism had not worked. Sakamaki wanted to turn back, but then he saw a huge wave carry off his crewmate Inagaki, and he himself was swept exhausted onto the beach, where he lost consciousness.

The second attack wave

The first attack wave commanded by Fuchida had not yet reached Pearl Harbor when a further 170 bombers and fighters from the *Kidō Butai* aircraft carriers north of Hawaii took off. This second wave, consisting of fifty-four Nakajima B5N torpedo bombers, eighty Aichi D3A dive bombers, and thirty-six Zeros, was led by Lieutenant-Commander Shimazaki Shigekazu. Born in 1908, Shimazaki was an experienced bomber pilot with a distinctive moustache. He had occupied various posts on the *Akagi*, *Kaga*, and *Sōryū* and had been involved in the bombing of Chinese cities during the Second Sino-Japanese War. In summer 1941, he had still been in command of Japan's fighter squadrons in southern China before being given command in September of the navy fighters on the *Zuikaku*.

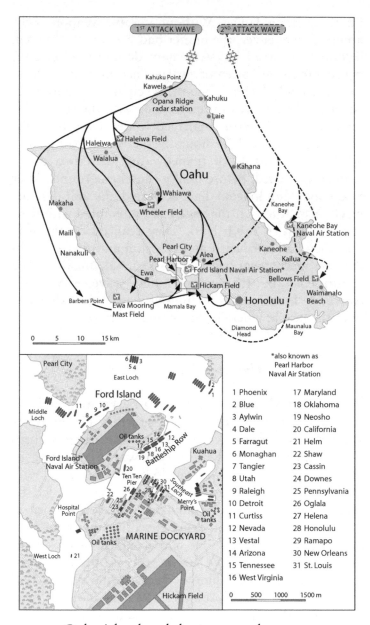

Oahu island and the two attack waves.
© Peter Palm, Berlin/Germany

The idea of the second wave commanded by
Shimazaki was to continue the bombardment of Pearl
Harbor without interruption, so as to give the US air
forces no chance to react to the surprise attack.[30] But
the Americans had no intention of giving up without a
fight. The pilots had rushed to the burning aircraft and
jumped into the undamaged planes. At around 9 a.m.,
individual Curtiss P 36 and Tomahawk (Curtiss P-40)
fighters took to the skies. Shimazaki and his men, who
were approaching Oahu, were about to come up against
American resistance.

Only a few minutes before the first Japanese wave,
the destroyer USS Monaghan anchored at East Loch
had received the order to head south-west to the harbor
entrance to come to the assistance of USS Ward, which
had sunk a submarine in the early morning. After the
Monaghan's anti-aircraft batteries had first of all aimed
their fire at the Japanese attackers, it set course a few
minutes before 8.30 a.m. for the harbor entrance, "to
get out of that damn harbor as fast as possible,"[31] as
William "Bill" Burford, the Monaghan's captain, put
it. Shortly afterwards it received a radio message from
USS Curtiss, which was transporting seaplanes, that
it had sighted a submarine periscope in the harbor
and had immediately opened fire. Along with several
other American ships nearby, the Monaghan joined in
the hunt for the Japanese midget submarine, the Kō-
Hyōteki from the I-22 tender commanded by the leader
of the submarine squadron, Lieutenant Iwasa Naoji. He
had taken the opportunity in the early morning, when
the net had been lifted to let in the patrol boats Crossbill
and Condor, to slip into the harbor. Now the crew of the
midget submarine fired its two torpedoes at the enemy.
Neither hit the Condor or the Monaghan, but one hit
the Ford Island jetty. The submarine was damaged by
depth charges from the Curtiss and was surfacing. At
around 8.40 a.m., just minutes before Shimazaki gave

the second Japanese attack wave the signal to form up to attack, Captain Burford ordered the *Monaghan* to head at full speed for the submarine in order to ram it. The destroyer managed to hit the submarine, which was just under the surface of the water, but only grazed it. The *Monaghan* also dropped two depth charges. The huge explosion from its own bombs caused the bow of the ship, which was still going at full speed, to lift out of the water and go on to collide with a dredger moored nearby, sustaining slight damage. Shortly afterwards an oil film and then air bubbles appeared on the surface, indicating that the *Monaghan* had managed to sink the submarine. The destroyer continued on its way out of the harbor onto the open sea. When the midget submarine was salvaged, it was found to have "a five-inch hole in the conning tower that killed the captain. He was blown into a mass of crumpled steel."[32]

At around 8.30 a.m., the three destroyers *USS Aylwin*, *USS Dale*, and *USS Farragut*, which had been anchored with the *Monaghan* in East Loch, were ordered to leave the harbor immediately. The *Aylwin*, its anti-aircraft batteries firing non-stop, moved sluggishly through the water. A bomb exploded just 50 meters from the ship. As it picked up speed, a bizarre scene unfolded. Half of the crew, including the captain Robert H. Rodgers, had been on shore leave that weekend. Together with his senior officers, he now embarked on a motor launch to catch up with his own ship as it escaped from the air raid. The crew on board realized that a small launch with their captain aboard was approaching, but the duty officers feared a submarine attack and did not slow down as the ship made its way out onto the open sea. Captain Rodgers and his officers were unable to catch up with the *Aylwin* and were ultimately taken on board the destroyer *USS Chew*.[33]

A good hour after the first attack wave had fired on the Naval Air Station in Kaneohe Bay in the north-east

Gun crew during the Japanese attack on Pearl Harbor.
Courtesy National Archives, photo no. 12009016

of Oahu, a further thirty-six planes reached the airspace over the military airfield. On their wings was the red sun, symbol of the Japanese Empire. The second wave had begun. The twenty-seven Nakajima B5N fighters from the *Zuikaku* in Shimazaki's squadron had been ordered to destroy Hickam Field, while a second squadron of twenty-seven torpedo bombers was to head for Ford Island and Kaneohe. They were led by Lieutenant Ichihara Tatsuo, who had gained experience on three aircraft carriers before being put in command of the torpedo and horizontal bomber squadron on the *Shōkaku*. Eighteen Nakajima B5Ns from Ichihara's squadron now bombed the Kaneohe Bay runway and hangars and destroyed further aircraft. Nine fighters each from the sister ships *Hiryū* and *Sōryū* escorting Ichihara's squadron flew over the runway. The constant barrage from the lightly armored and hence particularly nimble Zeros sprayed the runway, and the pilots and ground crew had no option but to run for cover. One man was determined to resist, however. John William Finn from California, who worked as an ordnance man repairing the weapons on the reconnaissance planes stationed in Kaneohe, had still been in bed with his wife Alice when he heard the engine noise of the low-flying Zeros, as well as gunfire and explosions coming from the airfield a mile away. He set off in that direction without delay. The scene was chaos. He quickly reviewed the situation and set up a heavy-caliber machine gun in a free area in front of the hangars. He was completely exposed and an easy target for the approaching Japanese fighter pilots, but the position was also ideal for opening up anti-aircraft fire. It offered such a clear view of the attackers that Finn could often make out the pilots' faces. Ignoring the bombs exploding around him, he fired doggedly at the attacking planes. Even when he was wounded by shrapnel, he did not stop returning fire. He was later awarded the Medal of Honor, the highest military award, for his bravery.[34] He hit one of the Zeros, but it managed to limp back to the *Kidō Butai*. Iida Fusata, commander of the fighter squadron from the *Sōryū* and nicknamed "young lady"[35] on account of his shyness, was less fortunate. After a salvo from Finn's machine gun had hit his fuel tank, the plane began to lose fuel. Realizing that it would be impossible for him to return to the aircraft carrier, Iida radioed the fighter pilot Fujita Iyozō: "I can no longer make it back and put you in charge."[36] Then he attempted to direct his heavily damaged plane towards the hangars so as to cause the greatest possible damage when he crashed. He missed his target, however, and was killed as he crashed into a nearby slope. Apart from Iida Fusata, whose remains were transported back to his home after the war, nineteen Americans died in the attack on Kaneohe.[37]

The attack had reduced the Kaneohe airfield to

rubble; thirty-three Catalinas had been destroyed, and only three reconnaissance seaplanes survived unscathed, as they were on flights at the time of the attack. The attackers also suffered casualties on their return to the aircraft carriers. Four planes from the 46th Pursuit Squadron had taken off from Wheeler Field, which had been almost completely destroyed during the first wave. Lewis Sanders, commander of the Squadron, together with pilots John Thacker, Philipp Rasmussen, and Gordon Sterling, set out to chase the enemy aircraft. Sterling, who actually belonged to the 45th Pursuit Squadron and was an inexperienced pilot, spontaneously joined Sanders's group. Although he was flying an unfamiliar aircraft, he shot down a Zero over Oahu. Shortly afterwards his own P-36 caught fire and crashed. Sanders and Rasmussen shot down one further fighter and a bomber before they returned to Wheeler Field with Thacker.[38] Fighter pilot Fujita, whom Iida had put in command of his squadron, returned to the Sōryū, although a second plane from the squadron was shot down by a Grumman F4F. Ishii Saburō's plane survived the attack on Pearl Harbor, but the pilot got lost on the way back to the Sōryū and radioed for the coordinates of his aircraft carrier. As radio silence had been ordered between the planes and the carrier fleet, however, the ship was not allowed to return his call, since the enemy might have been listening and discovered the whereabouts of the fleet. In tears, the radio operator on the Sōryū had to ignore the cry for help and abandon his comrade. The last signal from the pilot to the Sōryū said: "My plane is lost. I am turning round to destroy myself."[39]

Apart from Iida's squadron, the fighter squadron from the Hiryū led by Nono Sumio also briefly attacked Kaneohe, after which the nine planes turned round and at 9 a.m. reached Bellows Field further to the south, which so far had been attacked only briefly by one Zero

at 8 a.m. Now, Nono's squadron strafed the reconnaissance and fighter aircraft on Bellows Field and the B-17
heavy bomber standing at the end of the runway. Two
Tomahawks from the 44th Pursuit Squadron were shot
down by the incoming Zeros as they tried to take off.

Without the Kaneohe and Bellows Field airfields to
attack, the twenty-seven bombers led by Shimazaki,
commander of the second attack wave, flew over the
mountains of Oahu. Escorted by nine Zeros from the
Zuikaku, the squadron turned around on the southern
coast of the island to approach Hickam Field in attack
formation. Shortly after 9 a.m., Shimazaki's bombers
carpet-bombed the hangars, crew quarters, and office
buildings, also accidentally hitting the church next to
the airfield, collateral damage in an attack aimed exclusively at military targets. Some of the bombs missed
their target and exploded on the training area and a
baseball field.

The nine Zeros, led by ace pilot Shindō Saburō from
the *Akagi*, also took part in the concerted attack on
Hickam Field.[40] They dived three times to fire on the
American planes and buildings. Although the anti-
aircraft batteries returned fire, they failed to hit any
of the planes. All of the aircraft from Shimazaki and
Shindō's squadrons returned to their aircraft carriers,
where the latter reported tersely but not without pride
to Genda: "Inflicted much damage."[41]

Egusa's dive bombers

According to the Japanese war plan, four dive bomber
squadrons consisting of seventy-eight planes commanded by Lieutenant-Commander Egusa Takashige
were to fly to the core area of Pearl Harbor during the
second attack wave to finally sink the US battleships,
rounding off Japan's first sortie. Egusa's planes were

meant to attack the harbor in four stages at five-minute intervals. Whereas the first attack wave had been able to benefit from the element of surprise, the four squadrons led by Egusa, who had commanded the fighter units on the *Sōryū* since August, would now have to contend with anti-aircraft fire from the still intact ships. As Battleship Row was engulfed in thick black smoke from the heavily damaged battleships, it was almost impossible for Egusa's pilots to target the ships in the harbor directly. Ultimately, the dive bombers, each with one 250 kg bomb on board, had no option but to dive down onto their targets as soon as they were sighted. Egusa discovered some ships from the US Pacific Fleet lying in dry dock in the navy shipyard that had been untouched by the first attack. These were the main targets of the Japanese dive bombers.

The Aichi D3A type 99 carrier-borne bombers first set on *USS New Orleans*, which on the morning of December 7 was waiting to be repaired. The bombs narrowly missed the heavy destroyer, from whose deck crew members shot in desperation at the bombers with rifles and pistols. By a miracle, the *New Orleans* escaped serious damage that day.

The two destroyers *USS Cassin* and *USS Downes*, and the battleship *USS Pennsylvania*, were in dry dock near Ten Ten Pier. Egusa's attention was drawn in particular to the battleship *USS Pennsylvania*, moored behind the *Cassin* and *Downes*. Unlike its sister ship *USS Arizona*, the *Pennsylvania* had remained unscathed in the first attack. When the dive bombers commenced their bombardment of the dry dock in the navy shipyard, a bomb landed between the two Mahan-class destroyers *Downes* and *Cassin*. A fire broke out, gaining intensity as a result of oil leaking from a tank that had been hit, and began to spread wildly. When the flames reached the ammunition chambers and explosives on the *Cassin*, the ship exploded, and the hull of the destroyer, jacked up in the dry dock, slipped from the keel-blocks onto the *Downes*, which was already severely damaged by the fire.

USS Shaw also took a serious hit shortly after 9 a.m. Three bombs had hit the bridge, and the destroyer was ablaze. The crew were forced to abandon ship because of the conflagration, which was to prove fortunate for them because shortly after 9.30 a.m., a few minutes after they had left the ship, there was a huge explosion in the forward ammunition chamber visible from the dock. The violence of the explosion tore out the hull, catapulting parts of the ship as far as Ford Island.[42]

The light cruiser *USS Honolulu* – named for the capital of Hawaii – was also anchored in the naval shipyard, when the hail of bombs from three dozen dive bombers, led personally by Egusa, crashed down on it. Apart from some dents in the hull, Admiral Kimmel's flagship cruiser miraculously withstood the attack. By contrast, shortly after 9 a.m., a 250 kg bomb from an Aichi D3A penetrated the casemate of the *USS Pennsylvania*, Egusa's main target. It killed the crew of an anti-aircraft gun. Fragments from the neighboring destroyers *Cassin* and *Downes* caused further damage. With three dozen wounded, fifteen dead, and fourteen missing, the battleship got off relatively lightly.

The first Japanese wave had also surprised *USS Blue*, which was anchored in Pearl Harbor bay. The destroyer had set out to sea immediately after the bridge had received the report of the torpedoing of *USS Utah*. The *Blue* had not yet reached the harbor entrance when the second wave arrived. A .50 caliber machine gun on board took aim at the attacking dive bombers, opened rapid fire and scored a hit. One of the Aichi bombers went into a tailspin and crashed into the stern of the nearby *USS Curtiss*. The sailors on the *Blue* cheered as a second plane was hit and crashed near Pearl City. A few minutes later, at 9.10 a.m., the *Blue* was sailing through the buoys marking the harbor entrance. It had reached the open sea, where it started its patrol and located an enemy submarine. A short time after it had started chasing it and dropped depth charges over the side, air bubbles were seen. The *Blue* had clearly hit its target and sunk the submarine.[43]

North-west of Ford Island, the light cruiser *USS Raleigh* was close to the *Utah*, which had already sunk. The first attack wave had caused severe damage to the *Raleigh* and it was listing heavily. After 9 a.m., low-flying bombers once again attacked the ship. One bomb hit it but exploded on the seabed. The crew managed with great effort to put out the fire that had started and to keep the ship afloat. As Robert Simons, the *Raleigh*'s First Officer, later reported, his anti-aircraft batteries brought down five Japanese bombers, although he also counted the plane that crashed into the stern of *USS Curtiss*, which had probably been brought down by machine gun fire from *USS Blue*. In spite of the hits and severe damage, the *Raleigh* crew suffered only a few injuries and no deaths.[44]

When Japan's fighter planes attacked Pearl Harbor bay for a second time, Battleship Row was in ruins. Where earlier in the morning nine battleships had been peacefully anchored and tended to by their unsuspecting crews, billows of black smoke now rose up, making it much more difficult for the pilots in the second attack wave and offering a certain amount of protection to the US warships from further bombing. A burning oil slick floated on the surface of the water around the demolished ships. In the morning air, the tangy sea breeze mixed with the smell of burning oil. The creaking of the sinking ships and the moans of the wounded sailors could be heard far and wide. *USS Oklahoma* had capsized, and the deck of *USS Arizona* had already disappeared underwater. Other ships were visibly damaged and listing heavily. The *Oklahoma*, which was anchored on the sea-side of *USS Maryland*, offered protection from torpedoes for "Old Mary," which had got off lightly after the first attack, having been hit by just two bombs. Jammed between the wreck of the *Oklahoma* and Ford Island, it was gradually making its way forward. Of all the ships in Battleship Row, the *Maryland* was the least damaged by the attack.

The repair ship *USS Vestal* had suffered considerable damage during the first attack and was listing. When the second wave arrived, it was still close to the destroyed *Arizona*. Some of its crew members were seriously injured, with burns and broken bones. A tug was towing the *Vestal* and maneuvering it out of the danger zone, but it was still in a critical state. Water continued to enter the ship through a hole in the stern, and the hull was listing increasingly to starboard. Several fires had broken out on board and continued to blaze. In order to rescue his ship, captain Cassin Young therefore had no choice but to run it aground. At 9.45 a.m., the *Vestal* ran onto a coral reef on Aiea beach, south-east of Pearl City. It was now not far from the place where the *Blue*, which had managed to escape, had been anchored a few hours earlier.[45]

In the first attack on Battleship Row, *USS Nevada* had been hit by a torpedo but managed to escape shortly afterwards. When the planes from the second attack wave arrived, the ship, which had taken on some of the crew of the *Arizona*, had crossed the channel between Ford Island and Ten Ten Pier but had not yet reached the harbor entrance. For Lieutenant Makino Saburō, leader of the fourth of Egusa's squadrons to take off from the *Kaga*, the opportunity was too good to miss. If he managed to sink the already damaged *Nevada*, it would block the harbor entrance, trapping all of the ships of the US Pacific Fleet. Makino's Aichi D3A bomber dived towards the *Nevada*. Bombs exploded and shrapnel pelted onto the side of the ship. Huge

USS Arizona in flames: 1,177 American sailors lost
their lives when the US battleship sank in less than
ten minutes.

Granger/Bridgeman Images

waves whipped up by the explosions surged danger-
ously over the deck, threatening to wash the sailors
overboard. With so many bombers approaching, First
Officer Francis Thomas considered the risk to be too
great. If the *Nevada*, which was now floundering in the
water, sank, the channel would be blocked and other
US ships would be unable to escape. Thomas therefore
headed back to the shore and at 9.10 a.m. ran the heavily damaged *Nevada* aground at Hospital Point with
over 100 wounded and fifty dead on board.

At 9.30 a.m., George A. Rood, captain of *USS St.
Louis*, ordered his crew to maneuver the ship out of the
danger zone. Rood, who had himself served on a submarine, knew only too well that a ship as large as the light
cruiser *St. Louis* was an easy target for any submarines

that were possibly lying in wait at the entrance to the
harbor. To reduce the risk of being hit by an enemy
torpedo, Rood ordered his helmsman to steer at full
speed through the southern channel. At a speed of
over 22 knots (more than 40 km/h) – three times the
authorized speed in the channel – the *St. Louis* headed
for the harbor entrance. In doing so, it severed the steel
structure in the channel designed to prevent enemy submarines from penetrating into Battleship Row. Rood
finally breathed a sigh of relief when, shortly after 10
a.m., the *St. Louis* passed the buoys marking the harbor
entrance. He thought that his ship was now safe, but he
had nevertheless rightly anticipated that Japanese submarines could be lying in ambush. Shortly afterwards
the lookout announced that two torpedoes were heading for the ship. The cruiser zigzagged at the maximum
speed of 25 knots (46 km/h) to avoid them. The evasive
action worked, and the two torpedoes smashed into a
sandbank, but then the crew of the *St. Louis* noticed a
gray shadow in the water. Was it a submarine? Depth
charges were dropped, and just a few seconds later the
shadow disappeared and was not sighted again. The *St.
Louis* finally reached the open sea intact. The attack on
Pearl Harbor ended in the same way it had begun, with
an attack on a Japanese submarine by an American ship.

Together with the other ships that managed to escape
from Pearl Harbor on the morning of December 7
– including the light cruisers *USS Phoenix* and *USS
Detroit*, which had been anchored next to the capsized
Utah – the *St. Louis* set off on patrol. This ad hoc
group was to look westward to see whether a Japanese
armada was sailing towards Oahu. To defend against a
feared landing by Japanese troops, the battleship *USS
Maryland* was also held in readiness for forty-eight
hours after the attack, despite having been badly damaged. Some intact aircraft took off to look for Japanese
attackers. After reports that an aircraft carrier had been

sighted to the south of the Hawaiian islands, the spontaneously formed armada of US warships set off to hunt
the *Kidō Butai* – in vain, because after the second attack
wave the Japanese carrier fleet had moved northward,
away from Hawaii, as planned, and hence in the oppo-
site direction to where the US ships were searching.[46]

4

Consequences

The aftermath

At 9.45 a.m. on the morning of December 7, 1941, the drama of Pearl Harbor was coming to an end. After Egusa's pilots had completed their bombardment of the harbor, they flew once again over Wheeler Field, Hickam Field, and Ewa Mooring Mast Field, where they offloaded their remaining ammunition. Until the end, Fuchida Mitsuo, who had commanded the first attack wave, circled above Pearl Harbor to review the scene so as to be able to give his superiors as accurate a report as possible. Because of the billowing smoke in the harbor, however, he had a difficult task. Only after the last Japanese aircraft had turned around did he head back to the carrier fleet, where the planes from the two attack waves landed between 10.30 a.m. and 1.30 p.m. Fuchida's was one of the last to return to the *Akagi*.

The *Kidō Butai* was soon able to ascertain that it had incurred far fewer losses than expected. Only nine aircraft – three Zeros, one Aichi D3A and five Nakajima B5Ns – and twenty airmen from the first wave had been lost. The second wave had cost twenty planes – six Zeros and fourteen Aichi D3As – and thirty-four lives, including Nishikaichi Shigenori. As was learned later, the fighter pilot from the *Hiryū* had been forced to land

150

US sailors among burning seaplanes on Ford Island, with an explosion on *USS Shaw* in the background.

Picture Alliance/AP

on the Hawaiian island of Ni'ihau and was killed by the locals. Around fifty aircraft from the *Kidō Butai* were damaged, of which 80 percent were repaired. By contrast, the five midget submarines and nine of their ten crew members did not return.[1]

Operation Hawaii had been a great success for the Japanese, but what damage had it caused to the Americans? The US Pacific Fleet had incurred heavy losses: eighteen ships had been sunk or damaged, in some cases badly, including three light cruisers (*Helena, Honolulu, Raleigh*), three destroyers (*Cassin, Downes, Shaw*), four other ships (*Curtiss, Oglala, Utah, Vestal*), and all eight battleships. Of the latter, the *Arizona, California,* and *Oklahoma* were sunk. The burning *West Virginia* was in danger of sinking, and the *Nevada* had run aground. The other three battleships had been hit, the *Pennsylvania* being only slightly damaged. The *Arizona* and *Oklahoma* as well as the former battleship *Utah* were lost for good. All of the other ships were merely put out of action. They were recovered after the attack, repaired and soon – in the case of the *Maryland* and *Tennessee* already in February 1942 – back in service. Even the *California* and *West Virginia* were in operation again in summer 1944.

The US aircraft, most still on the ground, were hard hit: 188 were destroyed and 159 were no longer serviceable. Although it was thought initially that they would have to be scrapped, 80 percent of them were eventually repaired.

After the attack on Pearl Harbor: firefighters attempting to extinguish the flames on *USS West Virginia*. It was repaired and recommissioned by the US navy in summer 1944, before the end of World War II.

Universal History Archives/UIG/Bridgeman Images

The toll on human life was the worst for the USA: 2,403 fatalities, including 2,008 from the navy, 109 from the Marine Corps, and 218 from the army. There were also sixty-eight civilian deaths, persons who had been in the military facilities at the time of the attack or were the victims of friendly anti-aircraft fire. Some were killed in Honolulu, which a Nakajima had bombed by mistake. There were also 1,178 injured.[2]

Back on the *Akagi*, Fuchida listened to the reports by the leaders of the various squadrons so as to fill out his picture of the American losses. Then he reported to the bridge of the carrier fleet flagship, where Vice Admiral Nagumo, commander-in-chief of the *Kidō Butai*, asked him in front of the assembled staff officers: "Commander, how did the battle turn out?"[3] With a firm voice, Fuchida replied: "Four battleships were sunk for certain. I saw it with my own eyes. One exploded, another listed to the side, I am quite sure. The other two ships will also sink to the seabed." Nagumo countered: "So, four battleships have been sunk for certain. What about the other four?" "I had little time to be absolutely sure, but I think three battleships were badly damaged. The eighth ship is not unscathed but was not badly damaged," said Fuchida, adding with conviction: "The aim was achieved as planned." After he had indicated on the map the other damage to the airfields, pointing out that all aircraft on the ground and half of the planes in the hangars had been destroyed, Nagumo asked the key question: "Do you think that the US fleet will be able to launch a counterattack from Pearl Harbor in the next six months?" "The battleships will scarcely be able to do so in the next six months," replied Fuchida.[4] Nagumo was visibly pleased. The mission aim had been achieved: according to Fuchida's information, the US Pacific Fleet had been neutralized and an early counterattack was unlikely. Japan was now in a position to secure the natural resources of south-east Asia and to force a negotiated peace.

But what was Nagumo to do now? He discussed the matter with his staff officers on the bridge of the *Akagi*. As Fuchida reported after the war, he – along with Yamaguchi Tamon, commander of the Second Carrier Division – had pressed for a third and fourth wave, boasting that he could destroy the oil tanks and shipyards in Pearl Harbor.[5] Fuchida might well have added this aspect to his account afterwards, when the outcome of the war and the mistakes made by Japan's military leaders were known. In fact, it was probably only during his interrogation after the war that he first realized that the destruction of the fuel tanks and shipyards, where the demolished ships were repaired relatively quickly after the attack, would have been very damaging. Unlike the American battleships and aircraft carriers, targets on the ground were of second-ary importance to the Japanese and were therefore largely ignored. Although the planes on the aircraft carriers were made ready to take off again, it was not for another attack on Pearl Harbor but to counter a possible retaliatory raid by the Americans on the *Kidō Butai*, which was thought to be a more probable scen-ario. It is therefore unlikely that serious consideration was given on the *Akagi* to a further attack on the oil tanks and shipyards – even if such an attack would have been strategically decisive, delaying the restora-tion of the American fleet in the Pacific for more than a few months. The Japanese were more concerned about protecting their own aircraft carriers from an air raid than an all-out attack on the US base. But the failure to neutralize the oil tanks and shipyards in Pearl Harbor turned out to be a fatal error. In spite of what actually happened, the scene as described by Fuchida, in which the idea of a third wave was considered, was included in the blockbuster film *Tora! Tora! Tora!* (1970) and became part of the American collective memory in that way.[6]

Fuchida was unable to tell Nagumo the whereabouts of the US aircraft carriers. He had not seen them, nor any American aircraft that might have taken off from them, and therefore presumed that they were on maneuvers on the high seas. In order to attack the aircraft carriers, which was in fact the main aim of Operation Hawaii, Genda suggested that the *Kidō Butai* remain in its current position for a few days. Nagumo was more defense-minded, however, and wished to avoid a confrontation with the American aircraft carriers and return his own fleet to Japanese waters. As his assessment was based on Fuchida's positive situation report, he considered that the *Kidō Butai*'s mission had been completed.

Nagumo did not want to risk losing his own aircraft carriers in a confrontation with the American ones. As higher losses, including aircraft carriers, had been factored into the plan, Nagumo regarded the attack on Pearl Harbor, particularly in view of Fuchida's report, to have been extremely successful. So as not to jeopardize this outcome, he preferred to move away from Pearl Harbor. On its way back to Japan, the fleet encountered very stormy weather from December 11 to 13. If the Americans had been able to attack at this time, it would have been almost impossible for the aircraft to take off from the ships and provide effective aerial defense. On December 16, Admiral Yamamoto detached the aircraft carriers *Sōryū* and *Hiryū*, the cruisers *Chikuma* and *Tone*, and two destroyers for the conquest of Wake Island – which proved to be much more difficult than expected – while the rest of the fleet returned to Japan.

After the war, fighter pilot Harada reported that the crew of the *Sōryū* was at first jubilant about the victory in Pearl Harbor. As he himself had been merely part of the escort and had not taken part directly in the attack, he listened with envy to the drunken boasts of the returning pilots that they had "sunk American battleships."[7] As the report circulated that there had been no US aircraft carriers in the harbor – the main target of the attack – and that they had not therefore been sunk, the mood became much more subdued. Unlike Vice Admiral Nagumo, who was not an experienced military strategist, some crew members were well aware of what this could mean for the course of the war. For the Americans, the aircraft carriers – which allowed for more mobile and flexible warfare, as had been demonstrated in the attack on Pearl Harbor, where a carrier fleet had been used more effectively than ever before – would be a most decisive weapon. The possibility of confronting and defeating the American aircraft carriers required that Nagumo and the Japanese decision-makers keep the *Kidō Butai* near Hawaii. Nagumo missed this opportunity in the wake of Pearl Harbor. The Vice Admiral's error consisted not only of failing to send a third attack wave, an option that was not even discussed. In terms of military strategy, it would not have been a bad idea to invade Pearl Harbor, as Lieutenant-General Short, commander-in-chief of the US army in Hawaii, had feared.[8] However, the *Kidō Butai* had neither the ground troops nor the necessary equipment, because Yamamoto's war plan had not provided for this option. To complete the military mission in the manner conceived by the commander-in-chief of the Combined Fleet, Nagumo, who was focused on the destruction of the US battleships, should have remained with his fleet near Hawaii so as to confront the American aircraft carriers. If Admiral Yamamoto had been on the spot, he probably would not have hesitated to order a search for the American aircraft carriers. No doubt happy not to have lost any of his own aircraft carriers, however, he relied, as so often, on the status reports of his subordinate officers. He therefore failed to order the commander of the *Kidō Butai* to remain at sea near Hawaii and to hunt for and engage the American aircraft carriers.

The USA enters the war

After Nomura and Kurusu had been dismissed by Secretary of State Hull on the afternoon of December 7, they hurried back to the Japanese embassy. It was here that the two diplomats, who had worked so hard to negotiate a peaceful settlement, heard for the first time about the attack on Pearl Harbor. When Kurusu entered his second-floor office, he was greeted by an old school friend, finance official Nishiyama, who had come to obtain final instructions for the New York lawyer Desvernine, who was to act as mediator in arranging the planned meeting with Roosevelt on December 10. Nishiyama looked gloomy and sad, however. He had also heard what had happened in Hawaii. The two friends were dismayed that Operation Hawaii had removed any possibility of achieving a last-minute diplomatic agreement.[9]

A crisis management team met at the White House on the evening of December 7, consisting of President Roosevelt and Secretary of State Hull, along with major political and military figures. They were clear that in view of the treacherous and unannounced attack on the US naval base, war would have to be declared. Regarding a declaration of war at the same time on the German Reich and Italy, Japan's allies in Europe, the American government decided to wait for the expected declaration of war by Hitler and Mussolini.[10]

While Japanese units launched further attacks on the US bases in Guam, Midway, and the Philippines, and submarines attacked American ships in the Pacific,

Roosevelt gave an incendiary speech the next day at a special session of Congress:

> Yesterday, December 7, 1941 – a date which will live in infamy – the United States of America was suddenly and deliberately attacked by naval and air forces of the Empire of Japan. . . . It will be recorded that the distance of Hawaii from Japan makes it obvious that the attack was deliberately planned many days or even weeks ago. During the intervening time the Japanese Government has deliberately sought to deceive the United States by false statements and expressions of hope for continued peace. . . . Always will we remember the character of the onslaught against us. No matter how long it may take us to overcome this premeditated invasion, the American people in their righteous might will win through to absolute victory.

The president, whose hopes over the previous months for a peaceful settlement to the conflict with Japan had been destroyed, concluded with the appeal: "I ask that the Congress declare that since the unprovoked and dastardly attack by Japan on Sunday, December seventh, a state of war has existed between the United States and the Japanese Empire."[11]

The same afternoon, Roosevelt communicated to British prime minister Churchill the result of the vote in Congress: "The Senate passed the all-out declaration of war eighty-two to nothing, and the House has passed it three hundred eighty-eight to one. Today all of us are in the same boat with you and the people of the Empire and it is a ship which will not and cannot be sunk."[12] Jeannette Rankin, the first female member of Congress, was the only person to vote against the declaration of war on Japan. A confirmed pacifist, she had already voted years earlier against the USA's entry into World War I. With this one exception, Congress unanimously greeted Roosevelt's speech, in which he described December 7, 1941, as "a date which will live in infamy," with thunderous applause. The drawn-out discussion as to whether the USA should enter the war was now over. In that regard, the events in Pearl Harbor had acted as a catalyst. The USA was now resolved to go to war not only against Japan but also in Europe – hence Roosevelt's words to Churchill. Shortly afterwards, the British Empire also declared war on Japan, after Japanese forces had set out to invade British Malaya at the same time as the attack on Pearl Harbor and also started an offensive against the British Crown Colony of Hong Kong a few hours later.

In Berlin, Adolf Hitler was "extremely happy at this development." According to his propaganda minister Joseph Goebbels, he was "highly delighted"[13] to hear of the attack by Japan and in particular the decision by the US Congress to declare war. Through the events at Pearl Harbor and the USA's declaration of war against Japan, the various alliances turned the war in Europe into a world war. Hitler wrongly assumed that as a naval power Japan would not only keep the US navy in check in the Asia-Pacific region but would also defeat it, so that the USA would not be able to intervene decisively in Europe on the side of Great Britain. The German Reich felt that the surprising and successful Japanese offensive in the Pacific would help with its own victorious conquest. Italy and Germany both officially declared war on the USA on December 11, 1941, after Hitler had already given the order in the night of December 9 – the earliest possible moment – to sink every American ship in the Atlantic. The fronts between the Allies – led henceforth, thanks to its economic and military superiority, by the USA – and the Axis powers were now clearly drawn. Japan's attack on Pearl Harbor not only marked the start of hostilities between the USA and Japan in the Pacific. Through the involvement of the USA, which waged war both in the Pacific and the Atlantic at Great

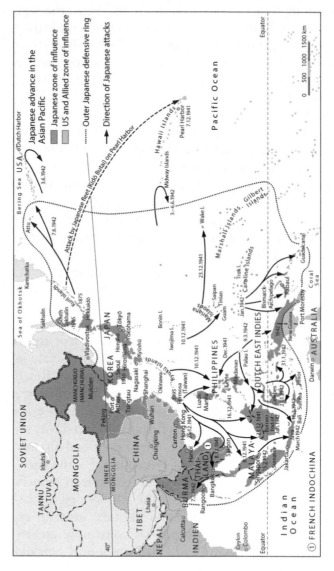

Japanese conquests 1941/42.
© Peter Palm, Berlin/Germany

Britain's side, the theaters of war in Asia and Europe were connected. The events in Pearl Harbor thus precipitated a major global confrontation – World War II.

The first prisoner-of-war

Hours after the attack on the US Pacific Fleet in Pearl Harbor, Hawaii was still in a state of shock. On the morning of December 8, 1941 – while the clearance and salvaging work was going on, the wounded were being treated, and the dead buried – twenty-one-year-old corporal David Akui, a Japanese-American born on Hawaii, was patrolling with Lieutenant Paul Plybon on Waimanalo Beach, just a few kilometers south-east of Kaneohe Naval Air Station, which had been heavily bombed the day before. Plybon and Akui, who had joined the Hawaii National Guard in October 1940 and, in spite of his Japanese roots, spoke not a word of Japanese, discovered an unconscious man lying on the beach. It was Sakamaki Kazuo from the midget submarine *HA-19*, who became the USA's first Japanese prisoner-of-war. His crewmate Inagaki was found dead. As Sakamaki was soon to hear when interrogated, all of his other comrades in the midget submarines had died. None of the Kō-Hyōteki submarines returned from Pearl Harbor.

During their military training, Japanese recruits had been indoctrinated to believe that for imperial soldiers only one thing mattered: military victory and no retreat. Absolute obedience to their superiors was of paramount importance for a Japanese soldier. Individuality and personal sentiments were to be subordinated to the esprit de corps. The US ignored Sakamaki's corresponding wish during his imprisonment to be executed or allowed to take his own life so as to be able to die with honor. He was to remain in captivity until the end of the war.

Sakamaki had been unable to fulfill the soldierly duty propagated in Japan to die or commit suicide rather than to be captured by the enemy. As a consequence, the war propaganda in his Japanese home now tried to brand him, at least subliminally, as some kind of "outlaw." Only nine of the ten crew members of the five Kō-Hyōteki submarines were shown, for example, in a picture in the magazine *Shashin Shūhō* or in a well-known and widely distributed painting. On April 8, 1942, exactly four months after the attack on Pearl Harbor, the nine submarine crew members were given a state funeral in the presence of Prime Minister Tōjō. Because they had died a hero's death for their country and Emperor they venerated almost as gods in Japan during the war – and are still venerated today in ultra-nationalist circles. Sakamaki's comrades, described as "nine fallen soldiers, distinguished by their incomparable uprightness and loyalty,"[14] and celebrated as "war gods," were also the subject of books, poems, and songs, while prisoner-of-war Sakamaki received no mention. His portrait was missing from all pictures, his name was not cited, and his whereabouts were left unspoken. As *HA-19*'s self-destruction mechanism had failed, the midget submarine also fell into the hands of the Americans. It was examined initially by technical experts in the US military and was then exhibited for the rest of the war to promote the sale of war bonds. It was decorated with red, white, and blue ribbons and toured the country with the inscription "Remember Pearl Harbor." Instead of causing further damage to the US Pacific Fleet, it thus helped to finance the American war against Japan. After Sakamaki returned to Japan, he published a book about his experiences in American captivity in 1949 entitled *Horyo Daiichigo* [First prisoner-of-war].[15] He subsequently worked for decades for the vehicle manufacturer Toyota, and was manager of its subsidiary in Brazil from 1969

A painting of the nine crew members of the five midget submarines in Pearl Harbor, venerated as "divine warriors" (*ky gunshin*). Sakamaki Kazuo, the tenth crew member, is missing. He was captured by the Americans at Pearl Harbor. The painting can be seen today in the Museum of Maritime History on the island of Etajima.

Private Collection Peter Newark Military Pictures/Bridgeman Images

to 1983 before returning to Japan. At the request of his family, his death in 1999 at the age of eighty-one was not initially announced. Throughout his life he was stigmatized in Japan as the "first prisoner-of-war."[16] Whereas Japan's attack on Pearl Harbor was celebrated as the island state's most glorious victory, recalled every year until the end of the war in 1945, it also created a victim on the Japanese side in the form of Sakamaki Kazuo.

The Japanese-American victims of Pearl Harbor

As a result of the attack on Pearl Harbor, the US president and his government finally abandoned their isolationist stance. Not only in Congress but also among the population, there was unanimous support, which Roosevelt might not have been able to achieve without Pearl Harbor, for declaring war. Under the slogan "Remember Pearl Harbor," the government in Washington launched a widespread propaganda campaign to maintain national unity in favor of the war. The American economy was soon transformed into a war economy, and countless young men were recruited into the armed forces to fight and win the war against Japan and its allies. Shortly after December 7, thanks to the propaganda campaign and the media reports of the attack, practically every US citizen had heard of Admiral Yamamoto Isoroku. Whereas he was celebrated in Japan as a national war hero, a great war planner, and the strategic mastermind behind the attack, the war propaganda in the USA made him into Public Enemy No. 1, on whom the hate and desire for revenge of a whole nation was focused. On the cover of *Time* magazine in December 1941, for example, he was depicted as a threatening yellow gorilla with an ugly scowling face, above the title "Japan's aggressor: Admiral Yamamoto."[17] For the Americans, Yamamoto was the initiator of an insidious attack on the USA without a declaration of war. The communication that Nomura and Kurusu were unable to hand over on time on December 7, 1941, merely stated that Tokyo regarded the Japanese-American negotiations as having ended, but the thirteen-page memorandum did not in fact contain a formal declaration of war. It was only hours after the successful attack on Pearl Harbor that Emperor Hirohito placed his seal on the official declaration.[18] For that reason as well, the words "Pearl Harbor" came

"I am looking forward to dictating peace to the United States in the White House at Washington"
— *ADMIRAL YAMAMOTO*

What do YOU say, AMERICA?

In a letter to a friend, the Admiral Yamamoto commented sarcastically on the warmongering politics in his own country, saying that Japanese troops would have to occupy the White House to make peace with the USA. He wondered whether the warmongers in his country had considered this. To promote support for the war after Pearl Harbor, US propaganda altered Yamamoto's statement and put into his mouth the words: "I am looking forward to dictating peace to the United States in the White House at Washington . . . What do YOU say, AMERICA?"

akg-images/Pictures From History

to signify an insidious, unannounced surprise attack. It was even used as a verb, for example in the Allied intelligence reports with reference to a suspected surprise attack in December 1942 on the port of Vladivostok, that Japan would "Pearl-Harbor."[19]

As anti-Japanese feelings were running high in the USA after the shock of Pearl Harbor, and the media provoked the fear of an imminent Japanese invasion of American soil, Roosevelt's government was under great pressure to act. The end of March 1942 saw the start of the compulsory resettlement of Japanese-Americans, US citizens with Japanese roots, many of whom lived on the West Coast. Canada and Mexico also aligned themselves with Roosevelt's anti-Japanese policy. As a result, many *Nisei*, second-generation Americans with Japanese roots, were interned for the duration of the war and had their assets confiscated. It was not until after the war – in Canada not until 1949 in some cases – that they were allowed back to their American towns and villages. The 150,000 inhabitants of Hawaii with Japanese roots, a third of the population, were not interned, but even there Japanese-language newspapers were censored, schools in the Japanese community closed, and radios, cameras, and transmitters confiscated from *Nisei*, who were regarded as potential spies. For a time they were not allowed to join the armed forces. Eventually entire *Nisei* battalions were formed, but because of the fear that they might desert to the enemy they were sent to the battlefields of Europe. Thousands of people with Japanese roots were thus also Pearl Harbor "war victims."[20]

Could Pearl Harbor have been prevented?

Shortly after the attack, the question also arose as to who was responsible on the American side. Admiral

Kimmel, commander-in-chief of the Pacific Fleet, and Lieutenant-General Short, commander of the US army in Hawaii, were early targets. They were relieved of office on December 17, 1941. The next day, Roosevelt ordered an investigation committee to examine the greatest military disaster in the history of the USA. Its findings, announced in January 1942, stated that Short and Kimmel had not performed their military duty to defend the base. The armed forces had not been sufficiently combat-ready. Because of his excessive fear of sabotage, Short had made the mistake of grouping the army aircraft together on the airfields, making them easy targets for the Japanese air forces.

The investigation, which continued until the summer, found that both commanders had made a series of bad decisions. The measures taken to defend Pearl Harbor, the reconnaissance of the enemy, and the cooperation between the army and the navy in general were deemed inadequate. Warnings from Washington were ignored, and information was misinterpreted or not acknowledged. The army in particular was not sufficiently alerted. Even though the navy returned fire immediately, the armed forces in general were criticized for not taking retaliatory measures directly during the attack. Short and Kimmel were accused of failing in their duties. For a long time they were scapegoats for Pearl Harbor and were only posthumously rehabilitated in 1999.[21]

Apart from Short and Kimmel, the navy department and war department also came in for fierce criticism, since the intelligence services had failed to pass on important information directly to Hawaii. The Signals Intelligence Service (SIS), a special secret department of the US army, had managed already in 1940 to break the code for the "writing machine for Latin languages, model 97,"[22] the Japanese foreign ministry's encryption machine. The decryption of what the Americans called the "Purple Code" enabled the USA to read well over

90 percent of Japan's diplomatic messages throughout 1941. In the run-up to Pearl Harbor, it had practically full access to the *Gaimushō* correspondence and diplomatic content, including the correspondence between Nomura and the foreign ministry in Tokyo. To obtain detailed information about the Japanese war plans and to prevent the attack on Pearl Harbor, however, it would have had to decode the multiply modified Japanese navy code, which the Americans called "Code JN-25," since even the Japanese foreign ministry and Nomura and the embassy in Washington were unaware of the strategic plans of their own navy. The encryption methods used for JN-25 and Purple were quite different, however, and American cryptographers were unable to break the navy code to any great extent until early 1942.[23]

Members of the Japanese foreign ministry were aware of the possibility that US intelligence could intercept the correspondence between the Japanese embassy in the USA and the *Gaimushō*. It had already done so once before, during the Washington Navy Conference in 1921/22. Kameyama, head of the telegraph office in Tokyo, assured foreign minister Tōgō in autumn 1941, however, that the encrypted diplomatic communication was secure. For Tōgō and the foreign ministry, the breaking of the diplomatic code by the USA, which it only discovered after the war, was a huge embarrassment.[24]

The Americans were able to deduce from the numerous intercepted and decoded telegrams that the Japanese considered a war to be conceivable, but they contained no specific indications as to when, where, and how Japan planned to attack the USA. In July 1941, Captain Henri Smith-Hutton, US naval attaché in the embassy in Tokyo, informed his government that the Japanese navy was commencing maneuvers in the Ariake Sea on the west coast of Kyushu, in which air attacks on large warships were being simulated.[25] But at the time it was not known that these exercises were related to Pearl Harbor, nor were Operation Hawaii and Japan's entry into the war already fixed.

Within the Washington navy department intelligence service, Lieutenant-Commander Alvin D. Kramer headed a special department with ten members engaged in translating the intercepted and decoded Japanese telegrams. During the escalating diplomatic crisis between Japan and the USA, Kramer's department was working under extreme pressure. Towards the end of 1941, Kramer himself would spend up to sixteen hours a day in the office. Like its counterpart in the army, however, Kramer's department in US naval intelligence did not have enough personnel to deal with the growing pile of Japanese documents. Depending on the length of the communication and the language used by the correspondent, it could take anything from a few hours to several days to translate. Kramer's responsibility for quickly examining and selecting messages of importance was thus of decisive significance. He had to employ his staff as efficiently as possible to ensure that no important information escaped the intelligence service. In view of the quantity of intercepted communications, this was an almost impossible task: quite simply, Kramer's department was insufficiently staffed.[26]

A further problem experienced by the Americans was the lack of communication between the military operational level and the army and navy intelligence services. Admiral Harold R. Stark, Chief of Naval Operations, took little notice of the warnings from the US naval intelligence, whose work in any case he held in low esteem. The fact that in 1941 the leadership of naval intelligence changed three times – at the time of the attack on Pearl Harbor, Rear Admiral Theodore S. Wilkinson had been in office for less than two months – did nothing to improve the service's reputation and its standing within the navy department. The relationship between the military operational level in the US army and the SIS was no less problematic. While the service interpreted the destruction of codebooks in Japan's diplomatic representations in London, Hong Kong, Manila, Singapore, and Washington in early December 1941 as a clear warning signal, the US military did not pay adequate attention to the information from its intelligence.[27] Indications and information were thus often effectively ignored, even after they had been decoded by the intelligence service.

Little attention was paid, for example, to the information intercepted by the American secret service in Washington in November 1941 that the Japanese consulate in Honolulu had been instructed in the middle of the month to report twice a week on the position of the ships in the US Pacific Fleet in Pearl Harbor. The US intelligence also had information about the "winds" code sent by the *Gaimushō* to all diplomatic representations, to be used in the event of an "emergency" in which communication between the Japanese embassy in Washington and the government in Tokyo would be interrupted. The Japanese foreign ministry instructed its embassies to destroy their coding machines on receipt of a coded weather report broadcast on Japan's shortwave radio service indicating the impending cessation of diplomatic relations with the USA ("east wind, rain"), the Soviet Union ("north wind, cloudy"), or Great Britain ("west wind, clear").[28] The "winds" code was considered highly significant in the investigations into Pearl Harbor after the war and the research on codes, although its relevance could not be ultimately determined, since no coded message in the form of a weather report "east wind, rain" has been identified to date. In any case, it would only have indicated an impending cessation of diplomatic relations, from which a forthcoming declaration of war against the country in question could be inferred, but nothing else.

As Gordon W. Prange rightly notes, there is no reason why the *Gaimushō* should have sent the code in the case of Pearl Harbor to inform its embassy in Washington of the cessation of diplomatic relations, since the channels of communication between the embassy in Washington and the government in Tokyo remained open before, during, and immediately after the attack on Pearl Harbor. Thus there is still no clear evidence that Tokyo sent a "winds" code message to Washington that the US intelligence service intercepted but had not interpreted before the attack on Pearl Harbor.[29]

There can be no doubt, however, that in the run-up to the attack, the US intelligence and military leaders in Washington failed to correctly interpret the information provided and to draw the necessary conclusions regarding the Japanese war intentions – a decisive prerequisite for preventing Pearl Harbor. In discussions of how the attack could have been prevented, reference is frequently made to specific incidents. In March 1941, the American secret service knew from a report by the naval attaché in Tokyo about the boasting of former admiral Takahashi Sankichi that the Japanese navy was fully equipped for all eventualities and was invincible. A few weeks later, a further report by the naval attaché contained a statement by another retired admiral that a war at sea with the USA would culminate in attacks on the Philippines or Hawaii.[30] Apart from the Philippines and Hawaii, which were indeed attacked in December 1941, the admiral also mentioned San Francisco and Panama, which the Japanese military never targeted. These statements were interpreted by the US secret service at the time as unserious "saber-rattling." In the first place, they were made long before the Japanese had concluded their strategic war planning. Moreover, they were merely statements by arrogant old Japanese admirals who overestimated the strength of their own navy without having any hard facts at the time to back up their ideas.

The US government can nevertheless be criticized for having underestimated Japan for too long. In view of their own economic and military strength, the Americans believed they were safe from attack. They did not expect Japan, whose troops had become bogged down in their advance into China in 1941, to go onto the offensive against a country that was visibly superior to it. In particular, the American government massively underestimated the willingness of the Japanese military to take risks. Nor could the Americans conceive of the revolutionary strategy devised by Yamamoto for the attack on Pearl Harbor: the massive deployment of Japanese aircraft carriers with navy air force planes and midget submarines.

The leaders in the war ministry and navy department in Washington can also be reproached for having ignored, filed away, and forgotten until December a report by the US ambassador in Tokyo, Joseph Grew, stating that a well-informed Peruvian envoy had told him that "a surprise mass attack on Pearl Harbor was planned by the Japanese military forces in case of 'trouble' between Japan and the United States; that the attack would involve the use of all the Japanese military facilities."[31] In defense of the US secret service and military leaders in Washington, however, it should be emphasized that this information was just one of many communications. Moreover, it arrived at a time when diplomatic tensions between the USA and Japan were not running anything like as high as they were in December 1941. When Grew sent his report, Nomura was not even in Washington, and bilateral discussions had not started.

In December 1941, however, in view of the Japanese invasion of French Indochina that summer and the hardening of the negotiating fronts, both the USA and Great Britain suspected that Japan would venture a further expansion in the Pacific – even if not initially an attack

on US bases. On December 2, for example, just a few
days before the attack on Pearl Harbor, Churchill spoke
to his foreign minister Anthony Eden of his firm conviction that Japan would attack the British Empire or the
USA, although he did not expect an offensive before
spring 1942. He predicted that the Japanese would
advance into Thailand. In early December, Roosevelt
also anticipated a Japanese attack, albeit in south-east
Asia.[32] Neither the British nor the Americans believed
that Japan's navy would dare to directly attack the US
Pacific Fleet in Pearl Harbor. If the Japanese fleet were
to attack in the Pacific, they expected it to target territories with natural resources, notably the Dutch East
Indies.

With hindsight it is conceivable that the Americans
could have anticipated the attack on Pearl Harbor on
the basis of the intercepted and decoded Japanese telegrams. At the same time, the American government
massively underestimated Japan's army and navy, in
part because of racial misconceptions. A direct attack
on the highly equipped Pearl Harbor, the most important US base in the Pacific, appeared too risky, even
reckless, and thus highly unlikely. Without knowledge
of the Japanese navy code, which was not broken until
early 1942 and which was to play a decisive role in the
Battle of Midway, it would have been impossible for
the Americans to know the date, place, and strength of
the planned Japanese attack.

Conspiracy theories

Alongside the discussion on the question of American
responsibility for Pearl Harbor, a mythology also developed, including conspiracy theories.[33] Shortly after
Japan's attack and the entry into the war by the USA,
efforts were made to exonerate those who, through lack

of communication and inadequate sharing of information, had helped the Japanese to maintain the element of surprise. The US president himself also became a focus of attention as a rumor spread that he had been fully aware of the attack but had allowed it to happen so as to give the USA a good reason to enter into the war against the Axis powers. A comment by Roosevelt to Harry L. Hopkins, one of his closest advisers, on the evening before the attack on Pearl Harbor – with the knowledge of the Japanese reply to the Hull Note, he is said to have used the words "this means war"[34] – is taken as supposed proof of this idea. The published sources on this incident do not reveal any mention of Pearl Harbor or an impending attack on the US base, however.[35] In the decoded message, the Japanese government had merely said on the day before the attack that it considered the bilateral discussions to be terminated. This was not an official declaration of war. Roosevelt no doubt meant that both sides were heading towards war. The conversation provides no evidence that he knew of the attack in advance. He was just as surprised by it as everyone else in the government. The authorities may be criticized solely for sleeping on the intercepted information and not considering until the following day, December 7, how to react to the breaking off of negotiations. At this point, the information had not even been officially announced. Moreover, the end of diplomatic negotiations did not inevitably signal the start of war. And above all, the cessation of discussions was not a declaration of war.

In 1999, the journalist Robert Stinnett resurrected the conspiracy theory discrediting Roosevelt, which was welcomed in Japan but highly criticized in the USA.[36] According to Stinnett, Roosevelt knew that the *Kidō Butai* was heading for Hawaii, since the Americans had picked up radio communications from ships approaching Oahu that had not observed the radio silence. In his research, however, Stinnett overlooked the fact that radio messages had also been picked up by American listening posts suggesting that the Japanese carriers and battleships were stationed in Japanese waters and that the flagship *Akagi* was heading south but not in the direction of Hawaii. Stinnett also failed to take account of the fact that the US secret service was not able to read intercepted documents in the Japanese navy code (JN-25) until March 1942, after Pearl Harbor. The source material cited by him as proof was not decoded and translated into English until *after* the navy code had been broken and in some cases until after the war – long after the attack on Pearl Harbor.[37]

In view of the fact that, even nearly eighty years after the events, Japan has still not come to terms with the war to the same extent as other countries, a thesis legitimizing the attack still does the rounds – as demonstrated, for example, by the exhibition at the Yūshūkan war museum on the site of the Yasukuni Shrine (*Yasukuni Jinja*) in Tokyo.[38] According to this exhibition, Roosevelt's aim was to join Great Britain in the war against Nazi Germany. To do so he had to overcome the resistance of the isolationists in the US Congress who wished to keep the USA out of the war in Europe. Roosevelt expected that a provocation by Japan and an American-Japanese war would inevitably result in the declaration of war on the USA by Germany. This explained the sharp tone of the Hull Note with its maximum demand for a wholesale Japanese troop withdrawal from the Asian mainland. By ceding to this demand, Japan would have sacrificed the "fruits" of its territorial expansion policy and its protracted war with China. The "blood toll" by Japanese soldiers exacted in China would then have been completely in vain. Driven into a corner by the economic sanctions and the Hull Note, Japan had no choice but to go on the offensive against the USA. Through the attack on Pearl Harbor,

provoked by the Americans, and the subsequent declaration of war on the USA by Hitler, Roosevelt achieved
his aims by involving the country in the war "by the
backdoor." This theory clearly places the blame for
Pearl Harbor and the outbreak of the war in the Pacific
on the USA and its president – and enjoys particular
popularity in Japan for that reason.

In the early 1980s a further conspiracy theory spread
in which the British prime minister Winston Churchill
knew in advance about the Japanese attack on Pearl
Harbor but deliberately withheld the information from
Roosevelt so as to ensure that the USA would enter
the war against Hitler's Germany on the side of Great
Britain. The proponents of this theory claim that the
British intelligence service had made decisive progress
in breaking the Japanese navy code JN-25 before Pearl
Harbor – although even they had not been able to
decrypt everything.[39]

To this day, conspiracy theories involving Roosevelt
or Churchill have one main feature in common: they
lack any credible evidence. Despite this, conspiracy theories regarding Pearl Harbor are constantly revived and
new ones invented. The continued existence and development of such theories are the result of a number of
considerations. Many people fascinated by Pearl Harbor
still fail to understand today how Japan and its military
leaders were able not only to plan the surprise attack
without being discovered but also to implement it successfully. Conspiracy theories offer explanations for this
and allow errors or weaknesses of the Americans to be
covered up. They also provide a scapegoat and the possibility of assigning blame for Pearl Harbor to a single
person, such as Roosevelt. Some of these theories also
find an explanation for the USA being caught unawares
or losing control to the supposedly weaker Japanese
military. They claim that, as chief executive, Roosevelt
must have known in advance about the impending

attack on the US Pacific Fleet. He exploited the plan for his own purposes to create a situation that would enable the USA to enter the war. Conspiracy theories thus allow Americans to believe that they were always in control, keeping intact a belief in the omnipotence and infallibility of the USA as a world power. Moreover, the idea of supposed complicity – tantamount to treason – is also sensational and has a fascination in its own right for that reason. True to the motto "the bigger the scandal the better," stories claiming that of all people the British prime minister or the US president knew in advance about Japan's attack on Pearl Harbor are in great demand and sell well. In Japan especially, particularly in ultra-nationalist circles, conspiracy theories pointing the finger at Roosevelt are also welcomed as a way of diverting attention from Japan's responsibility for the event and the world war it provoked.

Operation K

Directly after the attack on Pearl Harbor, the Americans were fearful that Japanese troops would attack the US West Coast and could land in California or Oregon, which were not well defended.[40] As was soon to be seen, however, Japanese operations were limited to submarine attacks on American ships on the West Coast. On January 11, 1942, a Japanese submarine managed to torpedo the aircraft carrier USS Saratoga 800 km southwest of Hawaii. It was badly damaged but not sunk. After repair and modernization in Pearl Harbor, it was back in commission in summer 1942.[41]

Less than three months after the attack on Pearl Harbor, Japan attempted to make up for what it had failed to do on December 7, 1941. Through two reconnaissance flights – the first ten days after the attack on Hawaii, the second on January 5, 1942 – the Japanese navy had learned that the commanders of the US fleet were doing their utmost to repair their ships as rapidly as possible and make them combat-ready. In Admiral Yamamoto's new plan in mid-January, the repair work in the shipyards, which had remained relatively unscathed in the original attack, was to be obstructed as a further blow to American morale. For that purpose, two Kawanishi H8K long-distance reconnaissance seaplanes, used for the first time and subsequently nicknamed "Emilys" by the Americans, were to fly to Hawaii from Japanese air bases on the Marshall Islands, each with a ton of explosive, and bomb Pearl Harbor. Japanese submarines with kerosene and bombs were to wait at the Hawaiian island of French Frigate Shoals, 850 km north-west of Oahu, to refuel the aircraft. After a flight of over 3,000 km, the two "Emily" aircraft that had set off from the Marshall Islands arrived at the submarines for refueling in the early evening of March 3 and took off again a few hours later for the flight to Oahu.

In the night of March 4–5, 1942, the two "Emilys" were detected by US radar stations as they entered the Oahu airspace. As on December 7, however, incorrect conclusions were drawn from these observations and the planes were assumed to be American. US reconnaissance and fighter planes took to the air to make sure, but they were looking above all for the Japanese aircraft carriers from which they assumed the planes had taken off. US naval intelligence had registered submarine activity near French Frigate Shoals but had deemed it insignificant, as it was thought that an air raid could be carried out only from an aircraft carrier.[42]

Thanks to the heavy cloud cover, the flight altitude, and the American error, the two Kawanishi H8K planes reached their target undiscovered and dropped their bombs on Pearl Harbor. The results were not very effective, however, first because of black-out precautions to protect the US Pacific Fleet from air raids, and second because of the unfavorable weather. In contrast to December 7, 1941, the sky over Pearl Harbor in the night of March 4–5, 1942, was cloudy and rainy. As a result, the two Japanese pilots could not say how effective their mission had been as they had dropped their bombs, not accurately over Ten Ten Pier, where the ships were being repaired, but randomly over Pearl Harbor. Japanese newspapers reported massive destruction of the military sites with thirty dead and seventy injured, based on a US radio transmission, but in fact, apart from a few uprooted trees, Pearl Harbor had suffered no damage from the attack. The pilots had missed their target and dropped most of their bombs into the water. This second attack thus remains a small and widely forgotten episode in World War II. As the war progressed, Admiral Yamamoto and Japan's military leaders did not dare to venture another attack on Pearl Harbor.

Epilogue

Fuchida Mitsuo boarded a battleship in a bay near Tokyo on the morning of September 2, 1945, as a member of an official Japanese delegation.[1] He had celebrated the greatest victory of his military career on December 7, 1941, as leader of the first wave to attack Pearl Harbor. After almost four years of war with the USA, he was now taking part in a ceremony on the battleship *USS Missouri* that sealed his country's greatest defeat. With the capture of the Okinawa Islands by US forces at the end of June 1945, and after the two atomic bombs had been dropped on Hiroshima and Nagasaki in August, Japan was finally defeated after years of war and had agreed to an unconditional surrender.

An entire American armada had gathered in the bay alongside *USS Missouri*, so as to demonstrate the strength of the USA to the defeated enemy and to drive home the fact that Japan had taken up arms against a superior opponent. One of the US battleships at anchor, *USS West Virginia*, had been targeted by Fuchida on that fateful December day in 1941. Black smoke had billowed up from the damaged ship on that occasion, making visibility in Pearl Harbor worse. When Fuchida made his report on the bridge of the *Akagi* to Nagumo Chūichi, commander of the *Kidō Butai*, he was sure that the *West Virginia* was damaged beyond repair and would sink.

He had been wrong. Just four years later, Fuchida was relieved that the surrender ceremony did not take place on the *West Virginia* but on the *Missouri*. No doubt he would have found the act of surrender even more shameful otherwise.

"I am full of energy. It is war and we do not know what the future will bring. But there is no time now to think about it. In any event, it is time for Japan either to flourish or to go under," Admiral Yamamoto wrote in a letter to his family just a few days after the triumph of Pearl Harbor.[2] But the Japanese Empire flourished as a result of Pearl Harbor only for a short time. Yamamoto did not live to see the day that Japan "went under," to use his own words. Thanks to their decryption of the Japanese navy code in early 1942, the Americans knew of the admiral's flight route and were able to carry out Operation Vengeance on April 18, 1943 and shoot down his plane over the island of Bougainville in Papua New Guinea. The planner of Pearl Harbor and Japan's most important strategist was killed in the crash. It was not therefore Admiral Yamamoto whom Fuchida gazed at in admiration on board *USS Missouri* on September 2, 1945. Instead, he acknowledged the tall, khaki-uniformed US Admiral Chester W. Nimitz, who had replaced Admiral Kimmel as commander of the US Pacific Fleet after Pearl Harbor and subsequently proved to have been a very fortunate choice. As the representative of the US navy on the day of the Japanese surrender, Nimitz placed his signature on the historic document marking Japan's defeat and the end of World War II.

The campaign of winter 1941/42, starting with the successful attack on Pearl Harbor, had given Japan control of large parts of the Pacific. To secure this huge territory, a powerful fleet and above all aircraft carriers were of vital significance, as demonstrated a few months

Surrender of the Japanese aboard the *USS Missouri*.
Admiral Chester Nimitz, representing the USA, signs
the instrument of surrender.

after Pearl Harbor in the battle between American
and Japanese aircraft carriers in the Coral Sea in May
1942 and the Battle of Midway in June 1942. The four
aircraft carriers *Akagi, Kaga, Hiryū,* and *Sōryū* that
had proved themselves in the attack on Pearl Harbor
were once again in action in the Battle of Midway and
were all destroyed. The situation in the Pacific changed
completely as a result, as Japan was forced onto the
defensive. The USA became more dominant: thanks
to its economic superiority and equipment it was able
to enlarge its fleet and overtake Japan in terms of aircraft carriers and battleships. Many people in Tokyo
believed prematurely that Pearl Harbor would be decisive. But Vice Admiral Nagumo had relied too heavily
on December 7, 1941, on Fuchida's report and retreated
with the *Kidō Butai* in the belief that the US Pacific

Fleet had been delivered a blow from which it would not recover so easily. By a fateful coincidence, the US aircraft carriers had not been in Pearl Harbor on that Sunday morning. Far fewer American battleships were sunk or put permanently out of action than Fuchida had assumed. As the shipyards and oil tanks on Hawaii had survived the attack, the US navy in Pearl Harbor was able to recover quickly. Soon the USA once again had a powerful fleet in the Pacific and was able to steadily push back the Japanese navy. In spite of the evident victory in Pearl Harbor, the war was actually lost for Japan at the start of the Pacific campaign. Forcing the USA to negotiate for peace would have been possible, if at all, only if Japan had been much more successful in the war. Operation Hawaii had certainly delivered the more powerful USA and its Pacific Fleet a heavy blow on December 7, 1941, but it had not by any means destroyed it.

In retrospect, it is academic to ask whether, even without the attack on Pearl Harbor, the USA would have entered the war in Europe against the German Reich sooner or later. The fact remains that Pearl Harbor brought about America's entry into the war, linking the battlefields of Asia and Europe in a major global conflict. There is no doubt, however, that the entry into the war of a country as economically and militarily superior as the USA played a decisive role in the defeat of Japan in Asia and Nazi Germany in Europe. Pearl Harbor was therefore not only a key event but a turning point in World War II.

Notes

Prologue

1 Japanese names are written in the traditional style with the surname first. The participation of Akamatsu Yūji in the attack on Pearl Harbor is historically documented; see Kira Isami and Yoshino Yasutaka, *Shinjuwan kōgekitai taiin retsuden: Shikikan to sanka tōjōin no kōseki* [Biographies of members of the Pearl Harbor attacking force: the flight route of captains and participating crews] (Tokyo, 2011), p. 105; http://www.shiko ku-np.co.jp/national/life_topic/print.aspx?id=20 031207000110 (accessed, like all cited internet sources, on June 30, 2016). Otherwise the Prologue is a fictional reconstruction.

1 The Background

1 The conversations and documents in this chapter are based mainly on Cordell Hull, *The Memoirs of Cordell Hull,* 2 vols. (New York, 1948); James William Morley, ed., *The Final Confrontation: Japan's Negotiations with the United States, 1941* (New York, 1994); Papers relating to the foreign

relations of the United States (hereafter abbreviated as FRUS), Japan 1931–1941, vol. 2; Diplomatic papers 1941, vol. 4 (Washington, D.C., 1943); Nomura Kichisaburō, *Beikoku ni tsukai shite: Nichibei kōshō no kaiko* [As ambassador in the USA: recollections of the Japanese-American negotiations] (Tokyo, 1946); *The "Magic" Background of Pearl Harbor*, 8 vols. (Washington, D.C., 1977) (hereafter abbreviated as MAGIC). For the Japanese-American talks in Washington see "The US-Japan war talks as seen in official documents" on the Japanese National Archive internet site http://www.jacar.go.jp/english/nichibei. See also as background literature Eri Hotta, *Japan 1941: Countdown to Infamy* (New York, 2013); Ōsugi Kazuo, *Nichibei kaisen e no michi: hisen e no kokonotsu sentakushi* [The road to the outbreak of war between the USA and Japan: nine alternatives to inevitable war], 2 vols. (Tokyo, 2008).

2 On Nomura's appointment as Japanese ambassador to the USA and the start of his service, see Matsuoka Yōsuke Denki Kankōkai, ed., *Matsuoka Yōsuke: sono hito to shōgai* [Matsuoka Yōsuke: a biography] (Tokyo, 1974), pp. 901, 924ff.

3 The Chinese names of the time are used here rather than the Pinyin spelling, e.g. Nanking rather than Nanjing, Chungking rather than Chongqing.

4 Kobayashi Hideo, *Daitōakyōeiken* [Greater East Asia Co-Prosperity Sphere] (Tokyo, 1989), p. 21.

5 Hiratsuka Masao, *Yamamoto Isoroku non shinjitsu* [The truth about Yamamoto Isoroku] (Tokyo, 2011), pp. 111–12.

6 Iriye Akira, *The Origins of the Second World War in Asia and the Pacific* (London, 2003), p. 68.

7 Hotta, *Japan 1941*, p. 27.

8 Letter, Roosevelt to Nomura, November 6, 1929, in Nomura, *Beikoku ni tsukai shite*, n.p.

9 Letter, Roosevelt to Nomura, April 6, 1937, in Nomura, *Beikoku ni tsukai shite*. All further translations from Japanese by the author (TM).

10 For relations between Roosevelt and Nomura, see Nomura, *Beikoku ni tsukai shite*, pp. 3ff. Roosevelt's medical records indicate that he might have been suffering not from polio but from Guillain-Barré syndrome, at the time a little-known neurological disease; see Armond S. Goldman, Elisabeth J. Schmalstieg, Daniel H. Freeman, Jr., Daniel A. Goldman, and Frank C. Schmalstieg, Jr., "What was the cause of Franklin Delano Roosevelt's paralytic illness?" *Journal of Medical Biography* II (2003), pp. 232–40.

11 Matsuoka, *Matsuoka Yōsuke*, p. 924.

12 MAGIC, vol. 1, no. 16 (telegram 136, March 8, 1941), A-12; see also Nomura, *Beikoku ni tsukai shite*, pp. 36–7.

13 For this meeting on March 14, 1941, see MAGIC, vol. 1, pp. 10–11; Nomura, *Beikoku ni tsukai shite*, pp. 42ff.

14 Hull, *Memoirs*, vol. 2, pp. 992–3.

15 MAGIC, vol. 1, pp. 15ff.; ibid., no. 45 (telegram 233, April 17, 1941) and no. 46 (telegram 234, April 17), A-35ff.; Nomura, *Beikoku ni tsukai shite*, pp. 50–1.

16 Hull, *Memoirs*, vol. 1, pp. 898–9.

17 Ibid., p. 899.

18 For War Plan Orange, see Louis Morton, *Strategy and Command: The First Two Years* (United States Army in World War II series: *The War in the Pacific*) (Washington, D.C., 1962), pp. 24ff.

19 For the Plan Dog memorandum, see Maurice Matloff and Edwin M. Snell, *Strategy Planning for Coalition Warfare: 1941–1942* (United States Army in World War II series: *The War Department*) (Washington, D.C., 1999), pp. 25ff.

20 Ibid., pp. 13ff.
21 Mark M. Lowenthal, *Leadership and Indecision: American War Planning and Policy Process, 1937–1942*, vol. 1 (New York, 1988), p. 398.
22 Morton, *Strategy and Command*, pp. 79ff., on the Plan Dog memorandum pp. 81ff., on Rainbow 5, pp. 86ff.
23 Quoted in MAGIC, vol. 1, nos. 55–9 (telegram 244, April 20, 1941), A-44ff.
24 Ibid.
25 Expressed by Matsuoka at a meeting of leading Japanese politicians in the presence of the Emperor on September 19, 1940, quoted in Iriye, *Origins of the Second World War in Asia*, p. 116.
26 Matsuoka, *Matsuoka Yōsuke*, pp. 726ff.
27 Hitler's interpreter Paul Schmidt offers a vivid account of Matsuoka's state visit to Berlin in late March 1941, in *Statist auf diplomatischer Bühne* (Frankfurt am Main, 1961), pp. 526ff.
28 MAGIC, vol. 1, no. 263 (unnumbered telegram, March 10, 1941), A-141–2; also no. 280 (unnumbered telegram, April 1, 1941, A-147–8, and no. 181 (telegram 1, April 7, 1941), A-148.
29 Kido Kōichi, *Kido Kōichi nikki gekan* [The diary of Kido Kōichi, vol. 2] (Tokyo, 1981), p. 854, entry for February 1, 1941.
30 On the evening of his return, Matsuoka had an audience with the Emperor to report on his trip; see Kido, *Kido Kōichi nikki gekan*, p. 854, entry for April 22, 1941.
31 MAGIC, vol. 1, nos. 45–9 (telegrams 233, 244, and 239, all April 17, 1941), A-35ff.
32 Ibid., nos. 62 and 63 (telegram 253, April 26, 1941), A-47–8.
33 Matsuoka, *Matsuoka Yōsuke*, p. 955.
34 Ibid., pp. 952ff.

35 MAGIC, vol. 1, no. 68 (telegram 190, May 3, 1941), A-50–1.
36 FRUS, Japan 1931–1941, vol. 2, p. 412.
37 Ibid., pp. 420ff.; MAGIC, vol. 2, Appendix, nos. 8 and 9 (telegram 219, May 13, 1941), A-4ff.; Nomura, *Beikoku ni tsukai shite*, pp. 54–5; see also Hotta, *Japan 1941*, pp. 72–3.
38 MAGIC, vol. 1, no. 328 (telegram 308, March 26, 1941), A-171–2, and no. 376 (telegram 286, March 19, 1941), A-195.
39 Quoted in Hotta, *Japan 1941*, p. 111.
40 MAGIC, vol. 1, no. 100 (telegram 285, May 9, 1941), A-67.
41 MAGIC, vol. 2, Appendix, no. 46 (telegram 375, June 8, 1941), A-30.
42 As reported by the British ambassador Robert Craigie: The National Archives Kew [hereafter abbreviated as TNA], FO 371/27909, From Tokyo to Foreign Office, no. 878, May 27, 1941.
43 Kido, *Kido Kōichi nikki gekan*, p. 869, entry for April 18, 1941.
44 Ibid., p. 879, entry for June 6, 1941.
45 Ibid., p. 883, entry for June 20, 1941.
46 Ibid., p. 884, entry for June 21, 1941.
47 MAGIC, vol. 2, Appendix, no. 160 (telegram 396, July 23, 1941), A-91.
48 Hotta, *Japan 1941*, pp. 123ff.
49 MAGIC, vol. 2, Appendix, no. 167 (telegram 405, July 24, 1941), A-95.
50 Antony Best, *Britain, Japan and Pearl Harbor: Avoiding War in East Asia, 1936–41* (London, 1995), p. 163.
51 FRUS, Japan 1931–1941, vol. 2, pp. 527ff.; Nomura, *Beikoku ni tsukai shite*, pp. 77ff.
52 MAGIC, vol. 2, Appendix, no. 183 (telegram 132, July 26, 1941), A-103.
53 Quoted in James R. Arnold and Roberta Wiener,

eds., *Understanding U.S. Military Conflicts Through Primary Sources* (Santa Barbara, 2016), p. 204; for this Executive Order, see ibid., pp. 203–4.

54 Kenneth G. Henshall, *A History of Japan: From the Stone Age to Superpower* (Basingstoke, 2012), p. 124.

55 Claire Lee Chennault, *Way of a Fighter: Memoirs of Claire Lee Chennault, Major General, U.S. Army (Ret.)* (New York, 1949), pp. 12ff.

56 Henshall, *A History of Japan*, pp. 124–5.

57 Herbert Bix, *Hirohito and the Making of Modern Japan* (New York, 2001), p. 401.

58 Kido, *Kido Kōichi nikki gekan*, p. 895, entry for July 31, 1941.

59 Ibid., pp. 895–6.

60 See also MAGIC, vol. 2, Appendix, nos. 204–7 (telegram 433, July 31, 1941), A-113.

61 MAGIC, vol. 3, Appendix, no. 14 (telegram 663, August 7, 1941), A-10–11.

62 Ibid., no. 44 (telegram 709, August 18, 1941), A-28.

63 At a joint lunch, Roosevelt informed Viscount Halifax, Great Britain's ambassador in Washington, that he had clearly impressed this on Nomura; TNA, FO 371/17909, From Washington to Foreign Office, no. 3849, August 18, 1941.

64 MAGIC, vol. 3, Appendix, no. 20 (telegram 671, August 8, 1941), A-13.

65 Oka Yoshitake, *Konoe Fumimaro: Unmei no seijika* [Konoe Fumimaro: politician of fate] (Tokyo, 1972), pp. 104ff.

66 Hull, *Memoirs*, vol. 2, p. 1024.

67 Roosevelt to Viscount Halifax, TNA, FO 371/27909, From Washington to Foreign Office, no. 3849, August 18, 1941.

68 MAGIC, vol. 3, Appendix, no. 65 (telegram 739, August 23, 1941), A-39–40.

69 Ibid., no. 132 (telegram 788, September 6, 1941), A-74–5.
70 These guidelines are printed in Tōgō Shigenori, *Tōgō Shigenori gaikō shuki: Jidai no ichimen* [Tōgō Shigenori's diplomatic records: a view of the time] (Tokyo, 1967), pp. 191ff.
71 Gomikawa Junpei, *Gozen Kaigi* [The extraconstitutional imperial conferences] (Tokyo, 1984), p. 187; see also Bōeichō bōeikenkyūjō senshishitsu cho [Department of Military History at the National Institute of Defense Studies], ed., *Senshi sōsho* [Military history series], 102 vols. (Tokyo, 1966–79), here Daihonei Rikugunbu Daitōasensō kaisen keii [Army Department of the Imperial Headquarters: the circumstances of the outbreak of the Greater Asia War], vol. 76 (Tokyo, 1974), p. 88.
72 For explanations of the imperial conference and liaison conference, see Gerhard Krebs, *Japan im Pazifischen Krieg: Herrschaftssystem, politische Willensbildung und Friedenssuche* (Munich, 2010), pp. 45ff.
73 Kido, *Kido Kōichi nikki gekan*, p. 909, entry for September 26, 1941.
74 Hull, *Memoirs*, vol. 2, p. 1033.
75 MAGIC, vol. 3, Appendix, no. 261 (telegram 923, October 10, 1941), A-148–9.
76 Kido, *Kido Kōichi nikki gekan*, p. 912, entry for October 9, 1941; for the demands for withdrawal, see ibid., pp. 911–12, entry for October 7, 1941.
77 Gomikawa, *Gozen Kaigi*, pp. 203–4.
78 See Asada Sadao, "The Japanese Navy's Road to Pearl Harbor, 1931–1941," in *Culture Shock and Japanese American Relations: Historical Essays* (Columbia, 2007), pp. 137–73, here pp. 137ff., 159.
79 Ōsugi, *Nichibei kaisen e no michi*, vol. 2, p. 118.

80 Krebs, *Japan im Pazifischen Krieg*, p. 211.
81 Kido, *Kido Kōichi nikki gekan*, pp. 915–6, entry for October 16, 1941.
82 MAGIC, vol. 3, Appendix, no. 369 (telegram 941, October 13, 1941), A-153.
83 Hull, *Memoirs*, vol. 2, p. 1035.
84 As ambassador Grew was in close communication with Prime Minister Konoe. He had great understanding of the Japanese intentions behind the meeting, as private secretary Robert A. Fearey noted in his record of this contact: "My Year with Ambassador Joseph C. Grew, 1941–1942: A Personal Account," *Journal of American-East Asian Relations* 1 (1992), pp. 99–136, here pp. 105ff.
85 Kido, *Kido Kōichi nikki gekan*, p. 917, entry for October 17, 1941.
86 Best, *Britain, Japan and Pearl Harbor*, p. 176.
87 Joseph C. Grew, *Ten Years in Japan: A Contemporary Record Drawn from the Diaries and Private and Official Papers of Joseph C. Grew, United States Ambassador to Japan, 1932–1942* (New York, 1944).
88 MAGIC, vol. 4, Appendix, no. 2 (unnumbered telegram, October 20, 1941), A-1–2.
89 Ibid., no. 3 (unnumbered telegram, October 22, 1941), A-2.
90 Tōgō, *Tōgō Shigenori gaikō shuki*, pp. 160–1, 207ff.
91 See Grew's reports of September 29 and October 25, 1941, in FRUS, Japan 1931–1941, vol. 2, pp. 645ff., 698–9.
92 See Grew's report to the State Department of November 3, 1941, ibid., pp. 701ff.
93 See TNA, WO 208/1046, The Pearl Harbor Operation (Allied Translator and Interpreter Section, Supreme Commander for the Allied

Powers, Research Report No. 1), December 1, 1945, pp. 9ff.

94 Quoted in Hotta, *Japan 1941*, p. 227.

95 Quoted in Ōsugi, *Nichibei kaisen e no michi*, vol. 2, p. 163.

96 MAGIC, vol. 4, Appendix, no. 64 (telegram 751, November 9, 1941) and nos. 65, 66 (telegram 755, November 10, 1941), A-32ff.

97 Ibid., nos. 68–70 (telegram 757, November 10, 1041), A-32ff.

98 Ibid.

99 Ibid., nos. 76–9 (telegram 1070, November 10, 1041), A-36ff.

100 Ibid.

101 Ibid., nos. 110–12 (telegram 1090, November 14, 1041), A-56ff.

102 Kurusu Saburō, *Hōmatsu no sanjūgonen: Nichibei kōshō hishi* [35 years of futile efforts: the secret history of the Japanese-American negotiations] (Tokyo, 2007), p. 81; see MAGIC, vol. 2, Appendix, no. 216 (telegram 646, August 4, 1941), A-120.

103 Kurusu, *Hōmatsu no sanjūgonen*, p. 86.

104 On the signing of the Tripartite Pact, see ibid., pp. 84ff.

105 *The New York Times*, November 9, 1941, p. 1:40.

106 Kurusu, *Hōmatsu no sanjūgonen*, p. 88; see MAGIC, vol. 4, Appendix, nos. 133, 135–7 (telegram 1118, November 17, 1941), A-71ff.

107 Kurusu, *Hōmatsu no sanjūgonen*, pp. 86ff., 91ff.

108 Ibid., p. 48.

109 TNA, FO 371/27912, From Washington to Foreign Office, no. 5253, November 18, 1941.

110 See Hotta, *Japan 1941*, pp. 259–60.

111 For Plan B, see Kurusu, *Hōmatsu no sanjūgonen*, pp. 99ff.

112 Hull, *Memoirs*, vol. 2, p. 1069.

113 MAGIC, vol. 4, Appendix, no. 162 (telegram 812, November 22, 1941), A-89.
114 Akimoto Kenji, *Shinjuwan kōgeki zenkiroku: Nihon Kaigun – Shōri no genkaiten* [A detailed presentation of the Pearl Harbor attack: the Japanese navy – high point of the triumph] (Tokyo, 2010), p. 80; Best, *Britain, Japan and Pearl Harbor*, p. 191; Pearl Harbor Attack: Hearings in the Joint Committee on the Investigation of the Pearl Harbor Attack, Congress of the United States, Seventy-Ninth Congress, 39 vols. (Washington, 1946) (hereafter abbreviated as PHAJ), vol. 15, pp. 1878–9.
115 Viscount Halifax reported on Hull's visible exhaustion in TNA, FO 371/27913, From Washington to Foreign Office, no. 5426, November 27, 1941.
116 China had even demanded that the number of Japanese troops in the north of French Indochina be limited to 5,000; TNA, FO 371/27912, From Washington to Foreign Office, no. 5378, November 24, 1941.
117 Hotta, *Japan 1941*, p. 265; Ian Kershaw, *Fateful Choices: Ten Decisions that Changed the World, 1940–1941* (London, 2007).
118 The Chinese ambassador in London, for example, expressed his great concern to the British Foreign Secretary Anthony Eden; TNA, FO 371/27914, Mr. Eden to Sir A. Clerk Kerr, no. 298, December 2, 1941.
119 In a personal meeting in Chungking, Chiang Kai-shek informed the British ambassador Sir Archibald Clerk Kerr of his protest and its influence on the final version of the Hull Note; TNA, FO 371/27914, From Chungking to Foreign Office, no. 615, November 30, 1941.
120 On the Hull Note, see Iguchi Takeo, *Demystifying*

Pearl Harbor: A New Perspective from Japan (Tokyo, 2010), pp. 127ff.; Kurusu, *Hōmatsu no sanjūgonen*, pp. 107ff.

121 Quoted in TNA, FO 371/27912, Telegram from Ashley Clarke to the Foreign Office, November 18, 1941.

122 The Treaty was signed in 1922 by the USA, Great Britain, the Netherlands, France, Belgium, Portugal, Italy, China, and Japan (!).

123 Hull, *Memoirs*, vol. 2, p. 1085.

124 TNA, FO 371/27913, From the President to the former naval person, November 25, 1941.

125 Ibid., From the Foreign Office to Washington, no. 6462, November 26, 1941.

126 Ibid.

127 Kurusu, *Hōmatsu no sanjūgonen*, pp. 111ff.

128 Kido, *Kido Kōichi nikki gekan*, p. 925, entry for November 26, 1941; the eight former prime ministers were Wakatsugi, Okada, Hirota, Hayashi, Hiranuma, Abe, Yonai, and Konoe.

129 Ibid., pp. 926–7, entry for November 29, 1941.

130 Kurusu, *Hōmatsu no sanjūgonen*, p. 126.

131 On Desvernine, see Iguchi Haruo, *Unfinished Business: Ayukawa Yoshisuke and US-Japan Relations, 1937–1953* (Cambridge, 2003), pp. 157ff.

132 Kurusu, *Hōmatsu no sanjūgonen*, p. 126.

133 Raoul Eugene Desvernine, *Democratic Despotism* (New York, 1936).

134 Kido, *Kido Kōichi nikki gekan*, pp. 927–8, entry for November 30, 1941; see Krebs, *Japan im Pazifischen Krieg*, pp. 255ff.

135 Kido, *Kido Kōichi nikki gekan*, p. 870, entry for April 21, 1941.

136 Craig Shirley, *December 1941: 31 Days that Changed America and Saved the World* (Nashville, 2011), pp. 17ff.

137 Kurusu, *Hōmatsu no sanjūgonen*, p. 118; see, for example, *The New York Herald Tribune* or *The Washington Post* of November 30, 1941, to see how the media reported Tōjō's speech.

138 Ōsugi, *Nichibei kaisen e no michi*, vol. 1, p. 117.

139 For an explanation of the proverb, see the Kiyomizu-dera website, http://kiyomizudera.or.jp/yodan/vol1/index_2.html.

140 Shirley, *December 1941*, pp. 4, 14–15.

141 "Japanese Troops Drill with Parachutes," *The Boston Evening Globe*, December 2, 1941, p. 19. Kwangtung is Guangdong in the south of China, not to be confused with Kwantung (Guandong) in north-east China. See also similar speculations in *The Washington Evening Star* of December 3, 1941.

142 FRUS, Japan 1931–1941, vol. 2, pp. 781ff.

143 Francis L. Loewenheim, Harold D. Langley, and Manfred Jonas, eds., *Roosevelt and Churchill: Their Secret Wartime Correspondence* (New York, 1975), p. 162, n. 2; Shirley, *December 1941*, pp. 132–3.

144 The Americans communicated the contents of the letter to the British government, see TNA, FO 371/27914, From Washington to Foreign Office, no. 5652, December 6, 1941.

145 Ibid., no. 5651, December 6, 1941.

146 Grew, *Ten Years in Japan*, pp. 414ff.

147 MAGIC, vol. 4, Appendix, no. 241A (telegram 902, December 6, 1941), A-130ff.

148 Because of the new time zones introduced on June 8, 1947, Hawaii is now six hours rather than six and a half behind Washington.

149 Hull, *Memoirs*, vol. 2, p. 1095.

150 Ibid., p. 1096.

2 The Japanese War Plan

1 For the Japanese war plan, see also Genda Minoru, *Shinjuwan sakusen kaikoroku* [Recollections of the Pearl Harbor Operation] (Tokyo, 1998), pp. 11ff.

2 The *Kidō Butai* consisted originally of the aircraft carriers *Akagi* and *Kaga* (First Carrier Division), *Shōkaku* and *Zuikaku* (Fifth Carrier Division), and *Ryūjō* (Fourth Carrier Division).

3 Japan's navy often regrouped the fleet, a presentation of which would be complicated and confusing. Suffice to say that at the start of the Pacific War, the aircraft carriers *Hōshō* and *Zuihō* belonged to the Third Carrier Division and were stationed on the Japanese inland sea. The aircraft carrier *Ryūjō* was the flagship of the Fourth Carrier Division and took part in the attack on the Philippines and then in the Japanese Malaya operation. The Third and Fourth Carrier Divisions were not involved in the attack on Pearl Harbor.

4 The biography of Admiral Yamamoto is taken from Yamamoto Yoshimasa, *Chichi Yamamoto Isoroku* [My father Yamamoto Isoroku] (Tokyo, 2012); Watanabe Yukō, *Yamamoto Isoroku: Sengo 70nen no shinjitsu* [Yamamoto Isoroku: the truth 70 years after the end of the war] (Tokyo, 2015).

5 A short summary of Yamamoto's US experience is provided in Watanabe, *Yamamoto Isoroku*, pp. 63ff.

6 Yamamoto, *Chichi Yamamoto Isoroku*, p. 223.

7 Hiratsuka, *Yamamoto Isoroku non shinjitsu*, p. 125.

8 On this episode, see ibid., pp. 122ff.

9 Quoted ibid., p. 129.

10 Ibid., pp. 126ff.

11 A short expert review of the three scenarios can be

found in Akimoto, *Shinjuwan kōgeki zenkiroku*, p. 39.

12 The contents of this letter, which has not survived, is quoted here from Genda's memoirs, Genda Minoru, "Higeki Shinjuwan kōgeki" [A tragedy: the attack on Pearl Harbor], in *Bungei shunjū*, December issue (Tokyo, 1962), pp. 198–202, here pp. 198ff.; see also Genda's comments in *Shinjuwan*, pp. 12–13.

13 Gordon W. Prange, *At Dawn We Slept: The Untold Story of Pearl Harbor* (New York, 1981), pp. 26–7; see also Genda's own description of the war plans in Genda, *Shinjuwan*, pp. 11ff.; the American historian John J. Stephan also concludes that before the attack on Pearl Harbor there was no serious or detailed plan for the capture of Hawaii. Yamamoto and his staff briefly considered plans, which the admiral – who wanted to avoid using too few resources for too many targets (aerial attack and invasion) – quickly discarded. See John J. Stephan, *Hawaii Under the Rising Sun: Japan's Plans for Conquest after Pearl Harbor* (Honolulu, 1984), pp. 55ff., esp. pp. 81ff.; "Nihongun Hawai senryō zenbō" [Details of the plans of the Japanese army to capture Hawaii], in Hata Ikuhiko, Hantō Kazutoshi, and Yokoyama Keiichi, eds., *Nichibei kaisen to Shinjuwan kōgeki hiwa* [The secret story of the outbreak of war between the USA and Japan and the attack on Pearl Harbor] (Tokyo, 2013), pp. 282–98, here pp. 282ff.

14 For the Third Carrier Division, see note 3.

15 Hiratsuka, *Yamamoto Isoroku non shinjitsu*, pp. 132ff.

16 Akimoto, *Shinjuwan kōgeki zenkiroku*, p. 43; Hiratsuka, *Yamamoto Isoroku non shinjitsu*, p. 138.

17 Quote based on Akimoto, *Shinjuwan kōgeki*

zenkiroku, p. 44; Hiratsuka, *Yamamoto Isoroku non shinjitsu*, p. 140.

18 This episode is described in Hiratsuka, *Yamamoto Isoroku non shinjitsu*, pp. 146ff.; on the decision of October 20, 1941, see Bōeichō bōeikenkyūjō, *Senshi sōsho*, Daihonei Rikugunbu Daitōasensō kaisen keii, vol. 76, p. 187.

19 For the war plan, see ibid., pp. 297ff., Yamamoto's plan, pp. 329ff., and the further progress of the war with the USA, pp. 344ff.

20 For this phase of the plan of attack, see Akimoto, *Shinjuwan kōgeki zenkiroku*, pp. 44ff.

21 Ibid., p. 45.

22 Ibid., p. 54.

23 Details of Fuchida's life are taken from Fuchida Mitsuo and Nakata Seiichi, eds., *Shinjuwan kōgeki sōtaichō no kaisō: Fuchida Mitsuo jijoden* [Memoirs of the air force commander of the Pearl Harbor attack: autobiography of Fuchida Mitsuo] (Tokyo, 2010), pp. 23ff.; Kai Katsuhiko, *Shinjuwan no samurai: Fuchida Mitsuo – Dendōsha to natta Paru Hābā kōgekitaichō no shōgai* [The samurai of Pearl Harbor: Fuchida Mitsuo – the life of the future lay preacher and commander of the Pearl Harbor attack squadron] (Tokyo, 2008), pp. 15ff.; see here Fuchida's admiration for Adolf Hitler, pp. 77ff.

24 Akimoto, *Shinjuwan kōgeki zenkiroku*, pp. 72ff.; Harada Kaname, *Reisen (Zero faitā) rōhei no kaisō: Nankin. Shinjuwan kara shūsen made tatakai nuita saigo no ikishōnin* [Memoirs of a veteran Zero fighter: the last eyewitness to fight from Nanking and Pearl Harbor to the end of the war] (Tokyo, 2013), p. 138; Henshall, *A History of Japan*, p. 125.

25 Akimoto, *Shinjuwan kōgeki zenkiroku*, p. 72ff.; on the torpedo problem, see Genda, *Shinjuwan*, pp. 199ff.

26 For details of Duke Kahanamoku, see Ellie Crowe, *Surfer of the Century: The Life of Duke Kahanamoku* (New York, 2007).

27 Robert Asahina, *Just Americans: How Japanese Americans Won a War at Home and Abroad – The Story of 100th Battalion/442nd Regimental Combat Team in World War II* (New York, 2006), p. 29.

28 Prange, *At Dawn We Slept*, p. 403.

29 See PHAJ, vol. 14, p. 1328; Prange, *At Dawn We Slept*, pp. 402ff.

30 Akimoto, *Shinjuwan kōgeki zenkiroku*, p. 80.

31 Ibid., p. 78.

32 Ibid., pp. 77–8.

33 When the island of Formosa (now Taiwan) came under Japanese colonial rule in 1895, the 3,952-meter "new high mountain" Niitaka (*Niitakayama*) replaced Fujiyama as the highest mountain in the Japanese Empire.

34 Akimoto, *Shinjuwan kōgeki zenkiroku*, p. 80.

35 Ibid.; Fuchida, *Shinjuwan kōgeki*, pp. 130ff.; Harada, *Reisen*, p. 145.

36 Yoshikawa Takeo, *Watashi wa Shinjuwan no supai data* [I was a spy in Pearl Harbor] (Tokyo, 2015), pp. 138–9.

37 On Kühn, see ibid., pp. 122ff.

38 Ibid., pp. 85–6, 113–14; PHAJ, vol. 12, p. 262.

39 MAGIC, vol. 4, Appendix, no. 291 (telegram 123, December 2, 1941), A-151.

40 Akimoto, *Shinjuwan kōgeki zenkiroku*, p. 69.

41 Ibid., p. 77.

42 Prange, *At Dawn We Slept*, pp. 346ff.; Suzuki Takeshi, *Dotō no naka no taiyō* [Hope amid stormy waves] (Tokyo, 1969), p. 198.

43 Yoshikawa, *Watashi wa Shinjuwan*, pp. 137ff.

44 *USS Nevada* and *USS Oklahoma* were Nevada-class battleships. The *Nevada* had been launched

a few weeks before the start of World War I and, thanks to its new weapon technology and the very large guns, it heralded the era of large battleships in the US navy. The Nevada-class ships were the first to have triple main turrets.

45 There were reports of "aircraft mother ships" from which seaplanes flew reconnaissance missions. These ships had been refitted to carry aircraft and were thus predecessors of genuine aircraft carriers.

46 MAGIC, vol. 4, Appendix (telegram 254, December 6, 1941), A154–5; Yoshikawa, *Watashi wa Shinjuwan*, pp. 145–6; Fuchida Mitsuo spoke incorrectly in his memoirs of three *aircraft carriers* instead of three *submarine tenders* (see Fuchida, *Shinjuwan kōgeki*, p. 123), a detail that seems to have been simply accepted by many historians. The submarine tenders *USS Sumner* and *USS Pelias* were moored at the submarine base. Other ships were anchored there, one of which was no doubt thought by Yoshikawa to be a further submarine tender.

47 Yoshikawa, *Watashi wa Shinjuwan*, pp. 145–6.

48 The Japanese consulate in Honolulu reported to Tokyo on the same day that the *Lexington* had left Pearl Harbor on December 5; MAGIC, vol. 4, Appendix, no. 296 (telegram 252, December 5, 1941), A-153–4; see also Prange, *At Dawn We Slept*, p. 460.

49 See the book by Gordon W. Prange, who interviewed Fuchida several times after the war: *God's Samurai: Lead Pilot at Pearl Harbor* (Washington, 2010), pp. 34–5.

50 Akimoto, *Shinjuwan kōgeki zenkiroku*, p. 82.

51 All references to Sakamaki Kazuo in Sakamaki Kazuo, *Horyo Daiichigō* [First prisoner-of-war] (Tokyo, 1949), pp. 5ff.

52 On the Kō-Hyōteki, see Akimoto, *Shinjuwan kōgeki zenkiroku*, pp. 70ff.

53 Mark Felton, *The Fujita Plan* (Barnsley, 2006), pp. 24–5; PHAJ, vol. 13, p. 494, vol. 36, pp. 55–6, and vol. 37, pp. 1296, 1299; Prange, *At Dawn We Slept*, pp. 484–5.

54 Felton, *The Fujita Plan*, pp. 25ff.; PHAJ, vol. 13, p. 494, and vol. 36, pp. 56–7; Prange, *At Dawn We Slept*, pp. 495–6; on the discovery of the midget submarine in 2002, see http://archives.starbulletin.com/2002/08/29/news/story1.html; http://the.honoluluadvertiser.com/article/2002/Aug/29/ln/ln03a.html. Even today, researchers cannot agree which of the midget submarines the *USS Ward* sank; it was released from either the *I-18* or the *I-20* tender.

3 The Attack

1 For this chapter, see also Fuchida, *Shinjuwan kōgeki*, pp. 137ff.; Carl Smith, *Pearl Harbor 1941: The Day of Infamy* (Oxford, 2001), pp. 35ff.

2 The *hachimaki* had the inscription *hisshō*, "determined to win"; Fuchida, *Shinjuwan kōgeki*, pp. 136–7; Prange, *At Dawn We Slept*, pp. 490–1.

3 "Sengo no shōgen kiroku: Taiheiyōsensō (Besatsu takarajima 2363)" [Record of the last eyewitness account: the war in the Pacific], in *Takarajima* [Treasure Island], special issue 2363 (Tokyo, 2015), p. 14.

4 Harada, *Reisen*, pp. 122ff., 149ff.

5 PHAJ, vol. 27, p. 532.

6 Ibid.

7 PHAJ, vol. 10, pp. 5027ff.; vol. 18, p. 3015; vol. 22, pp. 220ff.; vol. 27, pp. 566–7; and vol. 29, pp. 2121ff.

8 Fukumoto Kazuya, *Kishū! Pāru Hābā* [Surprise attack! Pearl Harbor] (Tokyo, 1972), p. 86.

9 For Fuchida's approach to Oahu, see Fuchida,

Shinjuwan Kōgeki, pp. 137ff., esp. pp. 145ff. and 153ff.; on Murata, see Kira, *Shinjuwan kōgekitai taiin retsuden*, p. 42.

10 Shirley, *December 1941*, p. 137.
11 Smith, *Pearl Harbor 1941*, pp. 43ff.
12 PHAJ, vol. 22, p. 126.
13 Smith, *Pearl Harbor 1941*, p. 54.
14 Prange, *At Dawn We Slept*, pp. 506–7; Smith, *Pearl Harbor 1941*, p. 47.
15 PHAJ, vol. 22, pp. 594ff., Smith, *Pearl Harbor 1941*, pp. 47, 66–7.
16 Smith, *Pearl Harbor 1941*, p. 49.
17 Ibid.
18 The sinking of the *Arizona* cost the lives of 1,177 American sailors. Today the USS *Arizona* Memorial commemorates the attack and is the last resting place of 1,102 of the sailors; see https://www.nps.gov/valr/index.htm.
19 Smith, *Pearl Harbor 1941*, pp. 49–50.
20 Prange, *At Dawn We Slept*, p. 518; Smith, *Pearl Harbor 1941*, p. 50.
21 Robert K. Chester, "'Negroes Number One Hero': Doris Miller, Pearl Harbor, and Retroactive Multiculturalism in World War II Remembrance," *American Quarterly* 65/1 (March 2013), pp. 31ff. Doris Miller was on board USS *Liscome Bay*, which was sunk by a Japanese submarine on May 24, 1943, near the island of Makin in the battle for the Gilbert Islands (Operation Galvanic).
22 Patrol torpedo boat 23.
23 Smith, *Pearl Harbor 1941*, p. 48.
24 Ibid., p. 51.
25 PHAJ, vol. 22, p. 126.
26 Smith, *Pearl Harbor 1941*, pp. 53–4.
27 "Writer Learns Hawaiian Raid No 'War Game,'" in *The Atlanta Constitution*, December 13, 1941, p. 1.
28 Smith, *Pearl Harbor 1941*, p. 54.

29 PHAJ, vol. 23, pp. 898–9; Prange, *At Dawn We Slept*, pp. 511ff.
30 Kira, *Shinjuwan kōgekitai taiin retsuden*, pp. 29, 58.
31 Prange, *At Dawn We Slept*, p. 531.
32 PHAJ, vol. 32, p. 309; on this episode see Akimoto, *Shinjuwan kōgeki zenkiroku*, pp. 224–5; Felton, *The Fujita Plan*, pp. 27–8; Prange, *At Dawn We Slept*, p. 531.
33 See the reports by Rodgers of December 12, 1941, and January 4, 1942, at https://www.ibiblio.org/hyperwar/USN/ships/logs/DD/dd355-Pearl.html.
34 See http://edition.cnn.com/2009/US/09/15/finn.medal.of.honor/index/html; for decades, Finn, who died in 2010, related his personal view of the attack.
35 Kira, *Shinjuwan kōgekitai taiin retsuden*, p. 70.
36 Harada, *Reisen*, p. 158.
37 Ibid.
38 Michael Slackman, *Target: Pearl Harbor* (Honolulu, 1990), pp. 140ff.
39 See Harada, *Reisen*, pp. 158ff.; on December 7 every year, representatives of Japanese Buddhist organizations visit the crash site to commemorate Iida's death; see http://www.mcbhawaii.marines.mil/News/NewsArticleDisplay/tabid/6999/Article/538924/fusata-iida-wwiis-first-kamikazae-pilot.aspx.
40 For Shindō, see Kira, *Shinjuwan kōgekitai taiin retsuden*, p. 69.
41 Prange, *At Dawn We Slept*, p. 534.
42 See http://www.history.navy.mil/research/archives/digitized-collections/action-reports/wwii-pearl-harbor-attack/ships-s-z/uss-shaw-dd-373-action-report.html.
43 PHAJ, vol. 23, pp. 692ff.; see also the report by the commanding officer of USS *Blue*, N. F. Asher,

of December 11, 1941, at http://www.ibiblio.org/
hyperwar/USN/ships/logs/DD/dd387-Pearl.html#/
Asher.
44 See the report by the First Officer of USS *Raleigh*, R.
E. Simons, of December 13, 1941, at http://www.
history.navy.mil/content/history/nhhc/research/ar
chives/digitized-collections/action-reports/wwii-pe
arl-harbor-attack/ships-m-r/uss-raleigh-cl-7-action
-report.html.
45 See the report by the captain of USS *Vestal*, Cassin
Young, of December 11, 1941, at https://www.
history.navy.mil/content/history/nhhc/research/ar
chives/digitized-collections/action-reports/wwii-pe
arl-harbor-attack/ships-s-z/uss-vestal-ar-4-action-
report.html.
46 See the report by the captain of USS *St. Louis*,
George A. Rood, of December 10 and 25, 1941,
at https://www.history.navy.mil/content/history/nh
hc/research/archives/digitized-collections/action-re
ports/wwii-pearl-harbor-attack/ships-s-z/uss-st-lo
uis-cl-49-action-report.html.

4 Consequences

1 Akimoto, *Shinjuwan kōgeki zenkiroku*, p. 229;
Kira, *Shinjuwan kōgekitai taiin retsuden*, p. 34.
2 Akimoto, *Shinjuwan kōgeki zenkiroku*, p. 241;
PHAJ, vol. 12, pp. 35ff., vol. 22, pp. 60–1; Prange,
At Dawn We Slept, p. 539.
3 Fuchida, *Shinjuwan kōgeki*, pp. 175ff.
4 Dialogue in ibid., pp. 176–7; Kai, *Shinjuwan no
samurai*, pp. 110–11.
5 Fuchida, *Shinjuwan kōgeki*, pp. 178–9; Harada,
Reisen, p. 156.
6 Jonathan Parshall also thought that Fuchida's
account was reconstructed with hindsight; see

"Reflecting on Fuchida, or 'a tale of three whoppers,'" *Naval War College Review* 63/2 (2010), pp. 127–38, here pp. 128ff.; see also the Oscarwinning 1970 film *Tora! Tora! Tora!*

7 Harada, *Reisen*, p. 156.

8 PHAJ, vol. 22, p. 57.

9 Kurusu, *Hōmatsu no sanjūgonen*, p. 133.

10 Hull, *Memoirs*, vol. 2, p. 1099. The British ambassador Halifax states that Hull expected Germany and Italy to declare war that same evening; TNA, FO371/27914, From Washington to Foreign Office, no. 5668, December 7, 1941.

11 The text and a sound recording of Roosevelt's "day of infamy" speech, a key document in US history, can be found on the website of the National Archive: http://www.archives.gov/education/lessons/day-of-infamy.

12 Roosevelt to Churchill, December 8, 1941, in Loewenheim et al., *Roosevelt and Churchill*, pp. 168–9.

13 Joseph Goebbels, *Die Tagebücher des Joseph Goebbels: Im Auftrag des Instituts für Zeitgeschichte und mit Unterstützung des Staatlichen Archivdienstes Russlands*, hrsg. von Elke Fröhlich, Teil II, Diktate 1941–1945, vol. 2, October–December 1941 (Munich, 1996), p. 453.

14 Kokuritsu Kōbunshokan [National Archive of Japan], Tokyo (hereafter abbreviated as KK), Jōhōkyoku henshū, Shashin shūhō, Nihyakujūnigō (shōwa jūshichinen, sangatsu jūhachinichi [Press Office]), ed., *Shashin shūhō*, no. 212, March 18, 1942 (Tokyo, 1942).

15 Sakamaki Kazuo, *Horyo Daiichigō* [First prisoner-of-war] (Tokyo, 1949).

16 See Ulrich Straus, *The Anguish of Surrender: Japanese POWs of World War II* (Seattle, 2005), pp. 8ff.; on the state funeral of Sakamaki's nine

comrades, see KK, Jōhōkyoku henshū, Shashin shūhō, Nihyakujūnigō (shōwa jūshichinen, sangatsu jūhachinichi [Press Office]), ed., *Shashin shūhō*, no. 217, April 22, 1942. An extract from the weekly Japanese newsreel on the funeral on April 8, 1942, can be viewed on the NHK television channel website: http://cgi2.nhk.or.jp/shoge narchives/jpnews/movie.cgi?das_id-D000300482_00000&seg_number-001.

17 *Time: The Weekly News Magazine*, December 22, 1941.
18 Bix, *Hirohito and the Making of Modern Japan*, pp. 436–7; Kido, *Kido Kōichi nikki gekan*, pp. 932–3, entry for December 8, 1941.
19 See, e.g., TNA, HW1/1192, British intelligence report from Chungking to London (untitled), December 26, 1942.
20 Asahina, *Just Americans*, pp. 13ff.; Bill Yenne, *Rising Sons: The Japanese American GIs Who Fought for the United States in World War II* (New York, 2007), pp. 18ff.
21 For the investigations, see, e.g., TNA, ADM 199/1363, The Japanese Attack on Pearl Harbor 7/12/41: Report of the Findings of the Army Pearl Harbor Board and Navy Court Inquiry – Official Reports of the Secretary of War 1941–1945.
22 Japanese: "Kyū-nana-shiki ōbuninjiki."
23 Douglas Ford, *The Pacific War: Clash of Empires in World War II* (London, 2012), p. 39.
24 Tōgō, *Tōgō Shigenori gaikō shuki*, p. 165; the Japanese had been warned by Germany in May 1941 that Nomura's coded messages were being read; MAGIC, vol. 1, Appendix (telegram 71, May 3, 1941), A-52.
25 John Prados, *Combined Fleet Decoded: The Secret History of American Intelligence and the Japanese Navy in World War II* (New York, 1995), p. 163.

26 Roberta Wohlstetter, *Pearl Harbor: Warning and Decision* (Stanford, 1962), pp. 171ff.
27 Richard J. Aldrich, *Intelligence and the War against Japan: Britain, America and the Politics of the Secret Service* (Cambridge, 2000), pp. 73–4; Prados, *Combined Fleet Decoded*, pp. 166–7.
28 On the "winds" code, see Aldrich, *Intelligence and the War against Japan*, p. 86; Prados, *Combined Fleet Decoded*, p. 167; MAGIC, vol. 4, Appendix (telegrams 148, 149, both November 19, 1941), A-81.
29 Prange reaches the same conclusion in *At Dawn We Slept*, pp. 360–1.
30 Prados, *Combined Fleet Decoded*, pp. 162–3.
31 Hull, *Memoirs*, vol. 2, p. 984.
32 Aldrich, *Intelligence and the War against Japan*, pp. 83–4.
33 For this chapter, see also Takeo, *Demystifying Pearl Harbor*, pp. 142ff.
34 Prange, *At Dawn We Slept*, p. 475.
35 PHAJ, vol. 10, pp. 4559ff.
36 Robert B. Stinnett, *Day of Deceit: The Truth about FDR and Pearl Harbor* (New York, 1999).
37 See Takeo, *Demystifying Pearl Harbor*, pp. 142ff.
38 The *Yasukuni Jinja* enshrines not only soldiers and officers who have fallen fighting for Japan since the Meiji Restoration, but also the souls of those executed as war criminals after World War II – including the fourteen class A war criminals (for example, Prime Minister Tōjō Hideki, or Matsui Iwane, commander of the Japanese troops at the massacre of Nanking in December 1937–January 1938). Fierce discussion is provoked between Japan and its neighbors, particularly China and South Korea, but also within Japan itself, when Japanese politicians, especially prime ministers, visit the Yasukuni Shrine to pay their respects to

the dead. See "Nationaler Stolz versus historische Verantwortung," in Evelyn Brockhoff, Bernd Heidenreich, and Andreas Rödder, eds., *Der 8. Mai im Geschichtsbild der Deutschen und ihren Nachbarn* (Wiesbaden, 2016), pp. 107–20, here pp. 112ff. The Meiji Restoration or Reform (1868–1890) is the name given to the modernization of Japan after 1868 on Western lines with a constitutional government system. The Meiji Constitution came into force in 1890. The Emperor's power was formally reaffirmed and the shogunate abolished. The reform program covered all major areas of the Japanese state (justice, economy, military, etc.). See as an introduction, Gerhard Krebs, *Das moderne Japan 1868–1952: Von der Meiji-Restauration bis zum Friedensvertrag von San Francisco* (Munich, 2009), pp. 1ff.

39 Aldrich, *Intelligence and the War against Japan*, pp. 68ff.

40 On Operation K (*Kē-Sakusen* in Japanese), see Felton, *The Fujita Plan*, pp. 79ff.; Steve Horn, *The Second Attack on Pearl Harbor: Operation K and Other Japanese Attempts to Bomb America in World War II* (Annapolis, 2005), for planning see pp. 33ff.

41 See the damage report for *USS Saratoga* of January 11, 1942, at http://ibiblio.org/hyperwar/USN/War Damage Reports/WarDamageReportCV3/War DamageReportCV3.html.

42 Felton, *The Fujita Plan*, p. 82.

Epilogue

1 The information in the Epilogue is based above all on Prange, *God's Samurai*, pp. 174ff.

2 Letter of December 19, 1941, Yamamoto, *Chichi Yamamoto Isoroku*, p. 224.

Select Bibliography

There is a large corpus of literature about Pearl Harbor, particularly in Japanese. The following selection of secondary literature on the subject is restricted to works in English and German.

Albright, Harry, *Pearl Harbor: Japan's Fatal Blunder*, New York, 1988.

Aldrich, Richard J., *Intelligence and the War against Japan: Britain, America and the Politics of the Secret Service*, Cambridge, 2000.

Arroyo, Ernest, *Pearl Harbor*, New York, 2001.

Best, Antony, *Britain, Japan and Pearl Harbor: Avoiding War in East Asia*, London, 1995.

Bix, Herbert, *Hirohito and the Making of Modern Japan*, New York, 2001.

Boog, Horst, Rahn, Werner, Stumpf, Reinhard, and Wegner Bernd (eds.), *Der globale Krieg: Die Auswertung zum Weltkrieg und der Wechsel der Initiative 1941–1943 (Das Deutsche Reich und der Zweite Weltkrieg*, vol. 6), Stuttgart, 1990.

Clarke, Thurston, *Pearl Harbor Ghosts: December 7, 1941 – The Day that Still Haunts the Nation*, New York, 2001.

Clausen, Henry and Lee, Bruce, *Pearl Harbor: Final Judgment*, New York, 1991.

Cressman, Robert, Di Virgilio, John F., and Wenger, J. Michael, *"No one avoided danger"*: *NAS Kaneohe Bay and the Japanese Attack of 7 December 1941*, Annapolis, 2015.

Ford, Douglas, *The Pacific War: Clash of Empires in World War II*, London, 2012.

Grew, Joseph C., *Ten Years in Japan: A Contemporary Record Drawn from the Diaries and Private and Official Papers*, New York, 1944.

Horn, Steve, *The Second Attack on Pearl Harbor: Operation K and Other Japanese Attempts to Bomb America in World War II*, Annapolis, 2005.

Hotta, Eri, *Japan 1941: Countdown to Infamy*, New York, 2013.

Hull, Cordell, *The Memoirs of Cordell Hull*, 2 vols., New York, 1948.

Iguchi, Takeo, *Demystifying Pearl Harbor: A New Perspective from Japan*, Tokyo, 2010.

Iriye, Akira, *The Origins of the Second World War in Asia and the Pacific*, London, 2003.

Keegan, John, *The Second World War*, London, 1989.

Kershaw, Ian, *Fateful Choices: Ten Decisions that Changed the World, 1940–1941*, London, 2007.

Kido, Kōichi, *The Diary of Marquis Kido, 1931–45: Selected Translations into English*, Frederick, 1984.

Krebs, Gerhard, *Das moderne Japan 1868–1952: Von der Meiji-Restauration bis zum Friedensvertrag von San Francisco*, Munich, 2009.

Krebs, Gerhard, *Japan im Pazifischen Krieg: Herrschaftssystem, politische Willensbildung und Friedenssuche*, Munich, 2010.

Kurusu, Saburō, Clifford, J. Garry, and Okura, Masako R. (eds.), *The Desperate Diplomat: Saburo Kurusu's Memoir of the Weeks Before Pearl Harbor*, Columbia, 2016.

Loewenheim, Francis L., Langley, Harold D., and Jonas,

Manfred (eds.), *Roosevelt and Churchill: Their Secret Wartime Correspondence*, New York, 1975.

Lord, Walter, *Day of Infamy: The Classic Account of the Bombing of Pearl Harbor*, New York, 2001.

The "Magic" Background of Pearl Harbor, 8 vols., Washington D.C., 1977.

Matloff, Maurice and Snell, Edwin M., *Strategic Planning for Coalition Warfare: 1941–1942 (United States Army in World War II series: The War Department)*, Washington D.C., 1999.

Morgenstern, George, *Pearl Harbor: The Story of the Secret War*, New York, 1947.

Morley, James William (ed.), *The Final Confrontation: Japan's Negotiations with the United States, 1941*, New York, 1944.

Morton, Louis, *Strategy and Command: The First Two Years (United States Army in World War II series: The War in the Pacific)*, Washington D.C., 1962.

Nelson, Craig, *Pearl Harbor: From Infamy to Greatness*, New York, 2016.

Papers relating to the foreign relations of the United States (FRUS), Japan 1931–1941, vol. 2, Diplomatic Papers 1941, vol. 4, Washington D.C., 1943.

Pearl Harbor Attack: Hearings before the Joint Committee on the Investigation of the Pearl Harbor Attack, Congress of the United States, Seventy-Ninth Congress, 39 vols., Washington D.C., 1946.

Prange, George W., *At Dawn We Slept: The Unknown Story of Pearl Harbor*, New York, 1981.

Prange, George W., *God's Samurai: Lead Pilot at Pearl Harbor*, Washington D.C., 2010.

Sakamaki, Kazuo, *I Attacked Pearl Harbor*, New York, 1949.

Slackman, Michael, *Target: Pearl Harbor*, Honolulu, 1990.

Smith, Carl, *Pearl Harbor: The Day of Infamy*, Oxford, 2001.

Stephan, John J., *Hawaii Under the Rising Sun: Japan's Plans for Conquest after Pearl Harbor*, Honolulu, 1984.

Stille, Mark, *Yamamoto Isoroku*, Oxford, 2012.

Stinnett, Robert B., *Day Of Deceit: The Truth About FDR and Pearl Harbor*, New York, 1999.

Tōgō, Shigenori, *Japan im Zweiten Weltkrieg: Erinnerungen des japanischen Aussenministers 1941–42 und 1945*, translated from Japanese, Bonn, 1958.

Toland, John, *The Rising Sun: The Decline and Fall of the Japanese Empire 1936–1945*, Barnsley, 2005.

Van der Vat, Dan, *Pearl Harbor: The Day of Infamy – An Illustrated History*, Toronto, 2001.

Weinberg, Gerhard L., *A World at Arms: A Global History of World War II*, Cambridge, 1994.

Wels, Susan, *Pearl Harbor, December 1941: America's Darkest Day*, San Diego, 2001.

Zimm, Alan D., *Attack on Pearl Harbor: Strategy, Combat, Myths, Deceptions*, Philadelphia, 2011.

Zöllner, Reinhard, *Geschichte Japans: von 1800 bis zur Gegenwart*, Paderborn, 2006.

Index

Page numbers in *italics* refer to figures.

213

220   Index